"In ***Praying for Church Challenges that Different Churches Face***, Jim Harrell delivers an excellent look at who the real enemy is in church revitalization and renewal and why we need to be prepared for the battle. This is a wonderful reminder about just how significant the discipline of prayer is to the process of church revitalization. This work looks at the two chapters in the Book of Revelation dealing with the seven churches of Asia Minor. Dr. Harrell emphasizes seven types of church in the battle for revitalization and renewal. He defines these as: Loveless, Vulnerable, Drifting, Confused, Nostalgic, Non-Missional, and Worldly churches. In a day where prayer is seen as more of an add on exercise only done when one gets around to it, Harrell reminds us that prayer for revitalization is the hard work requiring continual effort. Prayer is the humbling of the church revitalizer as they realize without the blessings of God through daily prayer, renewal in a church is impossible. Jim declares that the lack of prayer betrays a deep underestimation of the strength and cunningness of Satan the true enemy. This is a great book to give out to your entire church leadership team. It will challenge them to be all in as they pray first and work second. Without the first, the second is inconsequential."

Tom Cheyney, Founder & Directional Leader
Renovate National Church Revitalization Conferences
The Renovate Group
Author of *Your First 120 Days in Church Revitalization and Renewal*

"Two of the most common mistakes we make is acting without a foundation of prayer, and praying without ever moving to action. Jim ties the two together in a robust and practical prayer framework that is a corrective for a church looking to get back to their calling, and a preventative for those who want to avoid going off-track. Jim's strategic thinking and heart for prayer explains why he's such an integral leader in New England and the revitalization movement."

Charles Galda, President of Vision England

"I am so thankful for this new book by Jim Harrell. We are constantly needing ways to help a stuck congregation discover where they are and move toward Revitalization. This thoughtful volume will help every person involved in a church hoping to revitalize to see both diagnosis of the problems and prayers for the cure."

Dr. Jim Singleton, Assoc Professor of Pastoral Leadership and Evangelism, GCTS.

"The church in America today has fallen prey of the lie prayer is unneeded—or at best, a secondary concern—in church revitalization efforts. Nothing could be further from the truth! In this book, the author points out the crucial role it plays in all church efforts, and why the Enemy will do anything he can to derail it. The lessons shared from the churches in Revelation are eye-opening and sobering. Read this book at your own peril; it will likely convict you and drive you to your knees for your own church, and others you know."

Dr. J. David Jackson, Replant Specialist, Northeast USA North American Mission Board, SBC
Author of *ReNEW: Traveling the Forgotten Path*

"God does not call us to lament, bemoan or critique the church of the 21st century—God calls us to PRAY for it. With easy-to-follow guides, the book in your hands will show you HOW. Fair warning however; as you pray for revitalization in your region, joyful awakening may begin dawning on you and the American church at the same time."

> **Steve Treash**, Ph.D., Pastor, Black Rock Church, Fairfield, CT

"Jim is passionate about church revitalization... and now he's provided a spiritual tool for where to begin. I'm already using this biblical lens to pray for my church and other churches... and even my own revitalization! Let the Spirit take His Word and ignite your frontline prayers for God's renewal across New England."

> **Dennis Gill**, Pastor, President of eNET

"In *Praying for Church Revitalization,* Dr. Jim Harrell sets out a refreshingly new and practical way to do the old-fashioned hard work of praying for local church renewal. He explains how the Seven Churches of Revelation 2 and 3 are archetypes for the patterns of theological shift and missional drift of so many declining churches. Using this valuable tool, pastors and their leaders can now diagnose the conditions of decline and pray to the Lord of the Church in specific ways for correction, healing, and restoration to spiritual health."

> **Rev. Dr Jack L. Daniel**, Pastor Emeritus Free Christian Church, Andover, MA

I'm grateful to God for the work of Jim Harrell and *Overseed*. And now I'm also grateful for this book, which is rooted firmly in the biblical text and written with a clear burden for the church in every place, and especially in New England. May the important challenge to pray for church revitalization be taken up by thousands of Christians, and may the Lord who walks among the lampstands be pleased to strengthen his churches and receive glory from them.

> **Stephen Witmer**, Lead Pastor, Pepperell Christian Fellowship; Co-founder, Small Town Summits

"Church revitalization is never a 'one size fits all' proposition. Unfortunately, too many pastors and leaders look for a simple plan that can be executed quickly and efficiently. Jim Harrell builds the case for discovering many unique situations using the model of the seven churches from Revelation 2 & 3, each with its own strengths and weaknesses. He then shows the imperative of prayer as the power behind all revitalization, lest we think that the experts alone are adequate to change deeply entrenched church cultures. This book will challenge your assumptions and provide convincing evidence that revitalization ministry is truly a work of the Holy Spirit."

> **Rick Francis**, Pastor, Coach and Consultant with the Cecil B. Day Foundation

Praying For Church Revitalization:

Overcoming Seven Challenges Churches Face

DR. JIM HARRELL

OverseedPRESS

Praying for Church Revitalization
Published by Overseed Press
Division of William & James Publishing
581 Washington St, #3
Easton, MA 02375 U.S.A

The website references recommended throughout this book are offered as a resource to you. These websites are not intended in any way to be or imply an endorsement on the part of Overseed Press or William & James Publishing, nor do we vouch for their content.

ISBN 978-1-940151-05-2
© 2021 Dr. James Harrell

Printed in the United States of America
First Edition 2021

For my wife Sharon, who has been a wonderful living example of what it means to be the bride of Christ.

Contents

Foreword

Looking for a book that will challenge both your head and heart? You have it in your hands. The Architect of the church who said, "I will build my church and the gates of hell will not prevail against it" is calling us to hear and act with His appropriate strategies to heal and revitalize His church.

Jim Harrell, who's worked for years in church revitalization, introduces us to the Master's call and method. Now working with cohorts of pastors across New England, he shares and unpacks what the Word clearly speaks.

If we will seriously consider a deep commitment to prayer and implement what Jesus says to the seven churches of Revelation, change will come! He promises it in His call to them and to us.

Not a quick fix but a clear and concise call to revitalization and renewal. Examine your church, examine your life! I heartily recommend you listen, pray, and implement what you hear in this clarion call.

Christ calls again.

Paul Johnson, New England Consultant
Cecil B. Day Foundation

1 | Praying for Churches

1 | Praying for Churches

A pastor once said to me, "Things have to be really bad before I feel the need to pray." I know in my own life there have been far too many seasons where prayer has been more of an add-on product. It is something I know I should do, if only I could get around to it.

The difficulty is that I did not really want to get around to it. Prayer is work. Prayer does not feel like I am doing much. Prayer is humbling.

Prayer can feel like a diet. It is a discipline that is good for me, but food looks much more enjoyable. Such thinking betrays a disconnect that prayer can have in my mind. Prayer ought not to be a task to accomplish, but rather part of my ongoing relationship with my heavenly Father.

In America, many Christians pray perfunctory, though genuine, prayers at meals and before religious meetings. But we are not likely to be seen as those who rely on prayer or fully trust in God.

Christians are often guilty of presuming upon God. We believe that if we are attempting to do what God has called us to do, He will bless it. And God in His grace often does. Our churches grow, people come to faith as the word is preached, and lives are transformed. The Psalmist says,

> Once God has spoken; twice have I heard this: that power belongs to God, and that to you, O Lord, belongs steadfast love.[1]

God is both able and kind to bless church ministries. Yet, if we look under the covers, the success is mixed. So many pastors and church leaders are tired. Church families and marriages are suffering. The Church is not demonstrating an abiding joy. Church attendees really do not seem all that different from their non-Christian neighbors.

Could the missing piece be prayer? In my younger days, I thought of prayer as an activity done by Christians who could not, or would not, do the work of the church. They were like David's men who stayed with the baggage.[2] They would share in the spoils, but they were not really doing very much. This is embarrassing, but true.

Lack of prayer also betrays a deep underestimation of the strength and cunningness of our enemy. Churches often have a self-confidence not rooted in reality. They simply choose not to worry about Satan.

Those who know their bible can point to Jesus' promise.

> And I tell you, you are Peter, and on this rock I will build my church, and the gates of hell shall not prevail against it.[3]

---

[1] Psalm 62:11-12a
[2] 1 Samuel 30:21-24
[3] Matthew 16:18

Why be concerned? Jesus wants the Church to stay focused on this rock, the gospel, and Satan will be defeated. Prayer is not even mentioned.

Yet ironically, it is Satan who tempts churches to solely focus on the ministry and skip the hard work of prayer. Peter did not understand this promise by Jesus to mean that prayer was optional. Rather, the apostles saw prayer as foundational for building the church on the gospel.[4]

There is a war going on. Prayer is critical because it is how we fight in a spiritual war. Churches thrive when they focus on fighting spiritual battles using spiritual means, not by fighting human battles using human means.

We need to remember that as the Holy Spirit is working to move the Church forward, Satan is also working to move it backwards. God sows but Satan scatters. God causes His plants to grow but Satan sows tares among the wheat. There is full-scale spiritual warfare going on.

The interaction between God, heavenly beings, and mankind is a mystery. God has not revealed much detail about how this war is being playing out in the heavenly realms. What God has made clear is there is a battle, and prayer is a critical weapon for winning that battle.

---

[4] Acts 6:4

Paul writes that we are to:

> Put on the whole armor of God, that you may be able to stand against the schemes of the devil. For we do not wrestle against flesh and blood, but against the rulers, against the authorities, against the cosmic powers over this present darkness, against the spiritual forces of evil in the heavenly places. Therefore take up the whole armor of God, that you may be able to withstand in the evil day, and having done all, to stand firm. .... praying at all times in the Spirit, with all prayer and supplication. To that end, keep alert with all perseverance, making supplication for all the saints, [5]

Paul saw prayerlessness as a serious problem. For Paul, prayer was not simply an addition to his ministry plans and strategies. Prayer was foundational to the ministry.

Central to Paul's prayer was the gospel. Paul prayed for people to see, encounter, and comprehend the Savior Jesus Christ with an increasingly greater depth as they peered into the gospel – to grasp that Jesus is the means of our justification (how we are saved) and is also the means of our sanctification (how we grow in our salvation). Believers are transformed into the image of Christ only as they grow in their understanding, trust, and love of Jesus.

In Paul's classic prayer in Ephesians 3:14-18, he asks God to grant the Ephesian believers to be strengthened with power in the inner man, so that Christ might dwell in their hearts

---

[5] Ephesians 6:11–18

through faith, so that they might comprehend all the nuances of Christ's love for them and become more like Christ.

Organizational structures and principles are needed in the Church, just as Israel needed to have governmental structures in place to be a nation. However, the government was never to be the focus, God was. The point of Israel's national status was so they might know God and reflect God to the world. In the same way, the Church is to know and reflect its Savior to the world.

This knowing God goes hand and hand with prayer. We see this so clearly in the Psalms. Life is meant to be lived with God. We live each day in dialogue with Him as we deal with the challenges we encounter. The good, the bad and the ugly of our lives are all meant to be the basis for an ongoing conversation with God, our Father.

To skimp on prayer is to skimp on encountering God. To skimp on prayer is to leave oneself more vulnerable to the enemy. To skimp on prayer is to rob the church of the empowerment needed for them to encounter Jesus, to grow to be like Jesus and to reflect Jesus to a lost world.[6]

Prayer is crucial. The church must be seeking God in prayer, consumed with a desire to know the living God and be constantly asking God to renew the church in His image:

> Lord, let me seek you by desiring you, and let me desire you by seeking you. Let me find you by loving you, and by loving

---

[6] Colossians 1:9-12

you, find you. With thanks I acknowledge that you have made me in your image that I may remember you, contemplate you, and love you. But this image has been so worn away eroded by faults, and shrouded by the smoke of sin, that it cannot do that for which it was made, unless you renew it and recreate it.[7]

Where does praying for churches fit with all this? The state of the church in 21st century is mixed. Some churches are doing well. Others are doing poorly. Most churches are in the middle, surviving but not really thriving. One thing is clear, all churches need our prayers!

How can we appropriately pray for churches? We cannot realistically know every church to determine what their individual prayer needs are. It's not practical. So, is there a better way? Is there a way of grouping similar churches together to help us with praying for them?

One common way of grouping churches together in the 21st century is through the lens of "life stage." That is, to determine the health of a church by correlating a church's lifecycle according to the lifecycle of a human being. Life progresses through birth, adolescence, young adulthood, maturity, aging, decline, and death. Fortunately, unlike human beings, churches do not need to die. They can adjust, make changes and re-enter the life cycle at a former stage.

While lifecycle analysis can be a helpful model in understanding churches, the scriptures take a different

---

[7] St. Anselm of Canterbury, bishop : *Proslogion*, p 93. (author's rendering)

approach. First, the bible identifies general needs that are common to all congregations. Secondly, the scriptures also groups churches into several classes that inform us about how to pray for each type of church.

Jesus himself, gives us a framework for how to group various churches together and how to pray for them in Revelation chapters two and three. Jesus speaks to seven different churches about their specific struggles and confronts them with their need for revitalization. In these two chapters, Jesus identifies the unique challenges that each of these seven churches encountered, which are representative of what different churches have faced throughout the centuries.

Revelation chapters two and three gives us a helpful lens by which to identify the health of a church. Jesus categorizes the seven churches from the reference point of the gospel. Each church had deviated in some specific way from the gospel and was thus experiencing decline. Each church had different characteristics and prayer needs.

There are some prayer needs that span across all types of churches. There are also specific prayers that are needed at different stages of a church's life cycle and for different types of churches. For example, the needs of a toddler are both similar and yet very different from those of a thirty-year-old. Some prayers are appropriate for any age and some are more relevant to a particular age.

So, how are we to pray for the general needs of all churches? Fortunately, there are many places in scripture that give us models on how to pray for all churches. The Lord's prayer is one example. Another is Paul's prayer in Ephesians 3:14-21, which focuses on asking God through the Holy Spirit to empower and transform believers in the inner man in the church.

Another model for praying for the church is Colossians 1:9–12. Paul is praying for the church to be filled with the knowledge of God's will, specifically for them to live out that knowledge and bear fruit. Paul asks God for those in the church to be strengthened with all His power so that they would be steadfast and patient, joyously giving thanks to Him.

Throughout the scriptures we learn that central to praying for churches is to make the gospel both the foundation and the content of your prayer. Prayer is a conversation with God. God speaks to us through His word, and prayer is our response to God. Biblical prayer assumes we are being moved by and are responding to thoughtful meditation on what God has said to us in scripture.[8]

Every doctrine of scripture is fodder for how to pray for a church. We need to pray for each person in the church who does not know Christ to come to Christ. We need to ask God for each believer to mature in Christ.[9] For each one to both comprehend and ground their life on each doctrinal truth of the scriptures, of which the death and resurrection of Jesus would be first and foremost.[10]

---

[8] Tim Keller, *Prayer*, 124.
[9] Colossians 1:28
[10] 1 Corinthians 15:1-8

For example, you could pray for the local church through the doctrinal foundations laid out in Romans 1 through 11:

- How both the irreligious and the religious have fallen short of God's glory.
- How salvation is by faith alone in Christ alone.
- The reality of the believer's new identity in Christ.

You might pray for the Holy Spirit to grab the imagination of believers and ask that these truths would stimulate each believer's faith to an ever deepening trust in God.

In a similar manner, every command of scripture should also inform our prayers. You could pray through the calls to action in Romans 12-16 for churches. Ask God for the church to be renewed in its thinking, to minister the gifts given by the Holy Spirit, to practically love each other, and so on.

The church is to live like Jesus and each believer is to make progress in living out the implications of the gospel. For them to respond daily to challenges of life by faith as they seek to live like Jesus. Ask God, by His grace, to change them from one degree of glory to the next.[11]

Peter lays out this mindset for us:

> Therefore, preparing your minds for action, and being sober-minded, set your hope fully on the grace that will be brought to you at the revelation of Jesus Christ. As obedient children, do not be conformed to the passions of your former ignorance, but

---

[11] 2 Corinthians 3:18

as he who called you is holy, you also be holy in all your
conduct, since it is written, "You shall be holy, for I am holy."[12]

The bible, in some regards, is our prayer list for each other and
for churches. The Puritans were great examples of using the
doctrines and commands of scripture in their prayers.

Here is one such prayer for a disciple's renewal:

> O my savior, help me.
> I am slow to learn, so prone to forget, so weak to climb;
> I am in the foothills when I should be on the height;
> I am pained by my graceless heart,
> > my prayerless days,
> > my poverty of love,
> > my sloth in the heavenly race,
> > my solid conscious,
> > my wasted hours,
> > my unspent opportunities.
> I am blind why light shines around me;
> > Take the skills for my eyes,
> > grind to dust the evil heart of unbelief.
> Make it my chiefest joy to study thee,
> > > meditate on thee
> > > gaze on thee,
> > > sit like Mary at thy feet,
> > > lean like John on thy breast,
> > > appeal like Peter to thy love,
> > > count like Paul all things dung.
> Give me increase and progress in grace so that there may be
> > more decision in my character,
> > more vigor in my purposes,
> > more elevation in my life,

---

[12] 1 Peter 1:13-16

> more fervor in my devotion,
>> more consistency in my zeal.
> As I have position in this world,
>> keep me from making the world my position;
> May I never seek in the creature
>> what can be found only in the creator;
> Let not faith cease from seeking thee until it vanishes is into sight.
> Ride forth in me, thou King of Kings and Lord of Lords,
>> that I may live victoriously, and in victory attained my end. [13]

Every doctrine and command of scripture should inform our prayers. Pray for churches to believe and live out what is on every page of the bible.

Let the bible teach you the vocabulary of prayer. In the same way that a child learns how to speak from listening to his or her parents, so believers learn how to pray from listening to the bible. The Psalms alone give us a great range of language, attitudes, and emotions for different types of prayer.[14]

Seasoned pastor Harold Senkbeil describes this kind praying as follows:

> We pray by means of the word. That is, the texts of scripture that formed the basis of the consolation in help we apply to the suffering soul we also weave into our prayer on the sole's behalf. All prayer is essentially answering speech; We as the children of God repeat back to him the word he is spoken to us.

---

[13] Arthur Bennett, *The Valley of Vision,* p 184.
[14] Keller, *Prayer,* 54-55, 59.

The first step in such word-based prayer is simply to echo what he has told us, repeating back to him what he has promised or commanded in that word. Then we thank him for that same promise or command, confess our sins against the world, and finally ask him to give or bless whatever he speaks of in that word.[15]

Fortunately, the scriptures themselves provide us with the content on what and how to pray for churches and their congregations.

Unfortunately, Satan is actively trying to weaken our churches, and his goal is to destroy EVERY church. In the next chapter, we will look at Satan's basic strategies for attacking churches and to learn how to pray more effectively against Satan and his schemes.

---

[15] Harold Senkbell, *The Care of Souls*, 106.

2 | The Enemy of Churches

2 | The Enemy of Churches

In Genesis chapter 2 the antagonist is introduced. The enemy of God's creation is Satan. God's enemy has on his agenda to steal, kill and destroy,[16] and this evil is focused on God's people. Satan does everything he can to keep someone from faith. If he fails, then he works diligently to stunt a believer's progress in the faith.

Believers began life blinded by Satan and members of his kingdom of darkness. God opens our eyes to His grace through the gospel message, and our hearts respond. By faith, we confess Jesus as our Lord and Savior. In response, God forgives our sins, rescues us from the domain of darkness and transfers us to the kingdom of light.[17]

Yet, we still live among those who dwell in the domain of darkness. Our sinful nature is still attracted to the kingdom of darkness and its ways. The promises of Satan are attractive and seem to make sense as to how we should live life. Prayerlessness makes us even more susceptible to these schemes of Satan.

The church is always drawn into being seduced by Satan to be conformed to the world.[18] We see this truth clearly in Jesus' words to the seven churches in Revelation. Jesus warns the churches to guard against the deception of moving toward either syncretism or separation.

---

[16] John 10:10
[17] Colossians 1:13-14
[18] Rom 12:2

The danger of syncretism is that the Church will accept and merge biblical doctrine with the world's philosophies. Often, the church's motive is to make the gospel appear more attractive to unbelievers by not causing offense or to minimize problems for believers as they live in the world. Unfortunately, this results in the church no longer looking or thinking differently than the world. The Church's God given mission of making disciples of all nations who look, live, and think like Jesus becomes compromised.

The danger of separation is that the Church prizes its own righteousness so highly that she attempts to separate completely from the world. Often, the motivation is to remain pure, but that motive is grounded in the false belief that evil is out there in the community and the only way she can remain pure is to isolate. But this is a truncated view of evil.

This view of evil misses the truth that sin also dwells within us. A separatist way of thinking leads the church to abandon the God given mission to go make disciples of all nations. Thus, the unfortunate result is the same as syncretism – a loss of gospel impact in the surrounding community.

Usually, the impetus for the church to move in one of these two directions is suffering. When the church is suffering, it finds herself attracted to Satan's false promise to make life easier for the believer. Satan's strategy begins with making life difficult for believers. Once they have suffered awhile, Satan offers them a short-term solution to the pain. However, Satan's solution also includes compromise, an embracing of some deviation from biblical teachings. He tempts those in the church to abandon the long-term biblical approach to life for short term relief.[19]

Satan has various way to apply pressure on a church to motivate it towards syncretism or separation. Central to all these schemes is an attack at the root of the church's unique identity in Christ so as to force compromise.

There are four common schemes of Satan referenced by Jesus in His words to the seven churches. We will focus on each of the churches in the following chapters. However, let us first look at how Satan attacks churches using the following:[20]

(1) **False Authority**: Install doubt that Jesus can be trusted
(2) **Relational Pressure**: Apply pressure from the community to "fit in"
(3) **Economic Hardship**: Make accommodation necessary to succeed financially
(4) **False Teaching**: Distort Jesus' teachings to promote ungodly thinking and behavior

Satan uses all four of these schemes to afflict the churches in the Book of Revelation.

First, there is conflict over authority. Who should be trusted? In the first century, the hostility from other religions and especially from the Jewish Synagogues undermined the church's trust in the authority of Jesus' message. The conflicting claims of authority caused these believers to

---

[19] 2 Cor 4:7-18
[20] David A. deSilva, "The Social Setting of the Revelation to John: Conflicts Within, Fears Without," 287.

question if Jesus' metanarrative[21] was truly better than the Jewish practice.

Thus, we need to pray for the Church to have confidence in God's revealed word and for it to have the fortitude not to let compromise affect biblical truth.

The second scheme of Satan in Revelation is relational pressure. For these seven churches, the pressure came from the Roman political imperial cult[22] and the trade guilds.[23] The prolific worship of false deities in both government and business made it difficult for Christians to maintain their political and business relationships.

For example, the trade guild ceremonies revolved around animal sacrifices to their patron deity and likely to the emperor. This religious sacrifice was then followed by a meal with the main dish of meat being served from the sacrifices to their false gods. To participate in the meal meant the believer would have to eat meat offered to idols. If Christian believers failed to participate in the meal, it would mean being left out relationally. Like today, many conversations and relationships were built around the meal table.

---

[21] Meta-narrative is the post-modern term for a culture's overarching way of interpreting the events and circumstances of life that provides the structure for people's beliefs and gives meaning to their experiences.

[22] Rome required worshipping the Roman Emperor as a god.

[23] The trade guilds were business organizations for those in a similar trade, such as weavers, dyers, shoemakers, doctors, teachers, painters, and other occupations. They were not like modern day unions defending employee against employers but rather were formed to both protect and promote the particular business interests of that trade.

Life is relational. People in the church naturally want friends and to be included in community life. God's call to holiness and faith often results in Christians being cast outside of certain relational circles because of what they will or will not do. It hurts to lose one's seat at the table of friends and the power brokers. Satan offers a short-term solution to that problem, just compromise!

The church has always needed prayer to have its relational needs met in Christ and to hold firm to its identify in Christ, despite the costs. James, the brother of Jesus, put it this way

> You adulteresses, do you not know that friendship with the world is hostility toward God? Therefore, whoever wishes to be a friend of the world makes himself an enemy of God.[24]

The church needs us to pray for it to have the desire for friendship with God, not the world.

Third scheme of Satan is an economic threat. It manifests itself as a motivation for Christians to compromise for pragmatic economic reasons. deSilva describes this ongoing tension:

> Membership in one or another guild was very important for economic survival, especially since the early Christianity was comprised largely of artisans and crafts-persons. The issue, of course, was how far one could compromise one's dedication to Christ as Lord for the sake of economic survival.[25]

---

[24] James 4;4
[25] David A. deSilva, "The Social Setting of the Revelation to John: Conflicts Within, Fears Without," 298.

People's livelihoods were on the line. Not playing ball with the guilds often had a severe economic impact.

The Church has always needed prayer to love God more than money. Jesus was very clear that we cannot love both God and money.[26] The Church is to pray to God for daily bread and believe that God will keep His promise to provide. Prayer is needed for the strength to refuse to worship at the altar of money.

The fourth scheme of Satan is the threat from false teaching that distorts the bible. This internal threat came from various factions inside the church. These factions sought to ground their accommodation to the world in biblical doctrine. Church members find it difficult to deal with the tension that comes when their life choices contradict what the bible commands. Often, the path of least resistance is to formulate new creative doctrines that change what the bible teaches rather than change their behavior.

We saw a current day illustration of this several years ago in the United Church of Christ. Rather than acknowledging their life choices were contrary to the scriptures, they changed their whole interpretive framework for understanding the bible, throwing out two thousand years of church theology. Rather than submitting to God's word as authoritative, they gave themselves carte blanc authority to change any part of the

---

[26] Matthew 6:24

33

bible with the slogan "God is still speaking, don't put a period where God has put a comma." The problem was that God had put a period where they wish He had put a comma. God wants the church to cherish and submit to what He actually said, not what we wish He said.

The Church has always needed prayer to understand and accept what the bible teaches by faith. People have had trouble submitting to God ever since Adam and Eve decided to disregard God's command in the Garden of Eden. Revelation admonishes the church not to "give in" to the "powers that be" because these present-day false teachings and the powers that stand behind them are temporary. They are simply Satan's schemes to deceive the Church. Rather, the church needs to respond in faith to the eternal Power, the Lord Jesus Christ, who stands at the heart of the community's biblical doctrine.[27]

Thus, we need to pray for the Church to weather the pressures of false authorities, relational demands, economic hardships, and false teachings. Pray that churches would refuse to conform to world. Ask God to grant His power to believers to maintain sound doctrine and adjust their lifestyles to be in conformity with Jesus and less with the world.

---

[27] David A. deSilva, "The Social Setting of the Revelation to John: Conflicts Within, Fears Without," 301.

The Church needs God to do what only God can do, change human hearts. One prayer in the book of Common Prayer puts it this way:

> Almighty God, you alone can bring into order the unruly wills and the affections of sinners: Grant your people grace to love what you command and desire what you promise; that, among the swift and varied changes of the world, our hearts may surely there be fixed where true joys are to be found; through Jesus Christ our Lord, who lives and reigns with you and the Holy Spirit, one God, now and forever. Amen.[28]

Each church needs the general prayer discussed both in this chapter and the previous chapter. However, not all churches are alike. There are also specific needs according to the context of each individual church.

This leads us to ask, "Just how unique are individual churches?" Do we have to have personal experience with a church before we know how to pray for it specifically? Or do churches naturally fall into some common categories that could inform how we pray?

Jesus' words to the seven churches in Revelation answer this very question. Jesus shares with us a general framework for praying for seven types of churches and their needs. Let us

---

[28] "Preface of Lent," *The Book of Common Prayer*, 219.

begin our journey to understanding and applying this more specific framework for prayer.

3 | Introduction to the Seven Churches

3 | Introduction to the Seven Churches of Revelation

The church is the bride of Jesus. Yet, often it is like the wife who, after being married for many years, has functionally drifted apart from her husband. She is still married. She still lives together with her husband. She goes through the routines of life with her husband. However, she is no longer emotionally enamored with him. The wife functions more like a roommate than a wife. In this state, what is the avenue back to a great marriage?

The Church is to be all about Jesus and deeply in love with Him. Unfortunately, being deeply in love with Jesus, does not often describe an individual church. It fails to be the reality in the life of many churches. So, how can this be remedied?

Like the wife described above, the church needs to re-encounter her husband, Jesus Christ. The church needs to reengage relationally with Jesus. As Paul describes for us in in Ephesians 5, Jesus loves His bride, sacrificed His life for His bride and actively pursues and engages His bride.

The Church, however, has often lost her love and respect for Jesus, her husband. She is no longing living for His good and perfect will. Instead, she focuses on her own will, her own desires and going her own way.

Living a separate independent life from Jesus has never worked well for the church. Throughout the ages, many churches eventually shift theologically and drift missionally. It typically starts internally at first, but the decline eventually becomes evident to everyone. A church cannot thrive apart from Jesus. Instead, she goes from being vibrant, to being functional, then decline, and eventually death.

The way forward is to re-engage relationally with Jesus as the loving head of the Church. This means committing to rebuilding the relationship with Jesus. The church must both listen to Jesus speak though his word and talk with Jesus through prayer. This relationship with Jesus is always missing to some degree in churches that need revitalization.

Additionally, the church needs to be empowered by the Holy Spirit to embrace her identity in Christ. She needs God's grace to be able to be a living witness to the world. Thus, she needs other believers and other churches to be praying for her.

Hopefully, as you read this book, your desire to pray for other churches is increasing. In New England, so many believers drive every day by a white steeple church sitting on the green in the center of their town. This is likely a church that was once a bright beacon for Jesus. Unfortunately, the light has become only a small flicker of a candle that is close to burning out.

Fortunately, death does not have to be the end result. Throughout the Old Testament, God reveals His desire to renew His people. It begins with prayer. God moves His people to pray. For us, rather than simply witnessing the demise of these struggling churches, we have the privilege of praying for them.

This leads us to the next question. How should we pray for the thousands of churches that need to be revitalized? What do we pray beyond, "Lord, please fix this church"? We can pray through the doctrines and appropriate commands of scripture for these churches mentioned in the previous chapter. We can also enhance our prayers by praying about the particulars facing each church.

Fortunately (and unfortunately) revitalization is nothing new to the Church. As soon as churches were planted in the first century, it was not long before they needed revitalization. While each church is unique, they also fall into identifiable patterns or categories. Once you understand the framework by which to categorize a church, you have a better idea of what to pray about for that church. We encounter this framework in Revelation two and three.

John, the apostle, is given a personal message from Jesus to seven key churches of Asia Minor near the end of the first century. All seven churches needed some type of revitalization. The individual situations of these seven churches gives us insight into the dynamics of how and why churches need revitalization today. Jesus words give us both a framework by which to understand a church as well as a pattern for how to pray for that type of church. One commentator puts it this way:

> These seven epistles ... were really messages to these particular churches, in view of their several conditions, to stir them up to hold fast what was right, and to a amend what was wrong, as also all other churches in like conditions.[29]

The seven churches are to be viewed as representatives of the various churches in the first century, and by extension, to all churches throughout the ages. Although they were seven real churches, they also represent seven types of churches.

All regular churchgoers know that churches have issues. The first churches were filled with heresy, schism, false doctrine, and depravity. The New Testament records for us the various disagreements, quarrels and discord found among the brethren. The history of the Church contains many accounts of corruption, defection, and a falling away from the faith. We should not be surprised to find the same is true of the church today.[30]

Fortunately, there are methods and practices for helping move churches toward better health. The answer to the root problem found in each of these churches that Jesus addresses in Revelation was Jesus Himself. The church had either drifted away from embracing who Jesus was or they had failed to

---

[29] Joseph Seiss, *Lectures on the Apocalypse*, Vol I, 51
[30] W. A. Criswell, *Expository Sermons on Revelation*, Vol 2, 46.

believe a key attribute of Jesus and His work. In short, each church had drifted away from Jesus and the Gospel.

In response, Jesus admonishes each church to stop the decline and overcome the worldliness that had crept in. Jesus gives to each church a promise contingent upon overcoming certain challenges to motivate the church toward a thriving outcome. Each promise is meant to stimulate their faith, for all overcoming by believers is accomplished by faith:

> For everyone who has been born of God overcomes the world. And this is the victory that has overcome the world, our faith.[31]

Each church in Revelation was encouraged to trust Christ and to respond in faith to Jesus' promise through missional engagement in their local context. The one common admonition to each of these churches was to overcome sin and thereby refuse to be conquered by the world. Each church had failed to grasp how deeply their sin was affecting their witness in the world.

Though it should go without saying, Jesus needed to remind believers that if they would repent and turn from their sin, the church will be a better witness for Christ. Central to the gospel message is confession, forgiveness, and repentance. This

---

[31] 1 John 5:4

theme of repentance permeates what Jesus has to say to each of these seven churches.

However, this call to repentance also came with a corresponding challenge. Once they repented of their sin and embraced Christ-like living, the church would suffer for it. Godly behavior would result in the church being persecuted by the world.

Jesus encourages the churches with the promise that godly living and faithful witness would result in the ultimate victory, despite the fact that it may be accompanied by a level of persecution. He called the churches to the same model of overcoming He followed, persecution followed by glorification. Jesus conquered the world by dying on the cross.[32]

Jesus was always clear that there was a price to be paid for following Him. He told his followers:

> If anyone would come after me, let him deny himself and take up his cross daily and follow me. For whoever would save his life will lose it, but whoever loses his life for my sake will save it. For what does it profit a man if he gains the whole world and loses or forfeits himself? For whoever is ashamed of me and of my words, of him will the Son of Man be ashamed when he

---

[32] Beale, *Revelation*, 269-270

comes in his glory and the glory of the Father and of the holy angels. [33]

In addition to common admonitions, Jesus' words to the seven churches in Revelation chapters two and three are individual in nature. Jesus speaks to the unique context of each church.

Jesus' addresses the personal needs of each church, yet these messages were not meant to be private. Rather, they were to be read by all churches, for Jesus' words were meant to be instructive for all believers throughout the ages. Jesus emphasizes this by concluding each message with these words:

He who has an ear, let him hear what the Spirit says to the churches.

Jesus' words in Revelation chapter two and three instruct us on how to diagnose problems in individual churches. They provide us with a framework for how to identify various types of churches. This in turn, informs us how to pray for a modern-day church with similar issues and a similar need to re-engage with the Lord Jesus Christ.

Revelation was most likely penned near the end of emperor Domitian's reign in AD 94 or 95.[34] According to Revelation 1:4,

---

[33] Luke 9:23–26

[34] The weightiest external evidence appears in Irenaeus, *Against Heresies*, book five, where Irenaeus places the work "near the end of Domitian's reign," which would have been near the beginning of his own lifetime. David A. deSilva, "The

the entire letter is the revelation of Jesus Christ given by an Angel to the apostle John. The letter portrays the current state of the church and at that time reveals the things that will take place in the future.

The book of Revelation begins with John seeing seven golden lampstands, and in the middle of the lampstands is the glorified Jesus Christ. Jesus is holding seven stars in his right hand.

After John describes in detail what he sees, Jesus explains to John what the stars and the lampstands represent.

Jesus says:

> As for the mystery of the seven stars that you saw in my right hand, and the seven golden lampstands, the seven stars are the angels of the seven churches, and the seven lampstands are the seven churches.[35]

Jesus holds the churches in His hands, and He is also in the midst of the churches. Jesus is a husband who both cares for his bride and is also present with her. Jesus holds his bride in His hands. Jesus is intimately close with her despite His

---

Social Setting of the Revelation to John: Conflicts Within, Fears Without," 273–274.
[35] Revelation 1:20

overwhelming greatness. He knows His bride. He can speak from firsthand knowledge about his bride.

His words to the seven churches are the words of a caring husband who knows the details of his wife's life and character. Jesus appreciates His wife but also seeks the best for her. He is compelled to address areas in her life that need correcting because He wants her to fulfill her greatest potential.

To accomplish this, Jesus is willing to have difficult conversations with his bride. He does not shrink back from bringing what needs to be talked about. Jesus is kind and caring but speaks honestly to His bride.

The seven churches of Asia Minor are Ephesus, Smyrna, Pergamum, Thyatira, Sardis, Philadelphia and Laodicea. They are located as show on the map below.

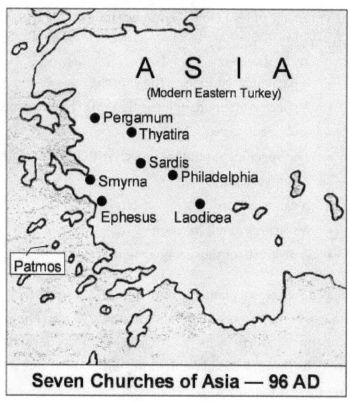

Seven Churches of Asia — 96 AD

36

These churches form a circle or a horseshoe around Asia Minor. They were all within one or two days' journey of each other, about twenty to thirty miles apart. The churches were in the same imperial province of Asia Minor, and hence under the same governor.[37]

36 http://fourcm.com/book-seven-churches-in-asia/
37 David A. deSilva, "The Social Setting of the Revelation to John: Conflicts Within, Fears Without," 273.

Each message of Jesus to the churches follows the typical pattern of:

- A particular address to the church
- A specific attribute of Jesus that this church is missing and needs to rediscover
- The specifics about this church with both a positive and negative critique
- A call to action
- A warning about inaction
- A promise for those who conquer

Each church was a planted from 50-60AD. They likely came into existence as a result of Paul's ministry in Asia Minor.[38] Now, thirty to forty years later, each church has developed its own culture and ways of ministering within the context of their local community.

Some of the developments in each church were certainly good, but some were negative. In some unique way, each church needed a course correction. Today, we would say that the churches needed revitalization.

Today, we still see these seven churches representing seven categories of churches found in the world.[39] Each church in

---

[38] Acts 19:10

[39] The epistles to these seven churches describe conditions which occur not in one particular age of the Church History, but again and again. William Henrickson, *More than Conquerors*, 60.

Revelation was struggling in different ways to be the church that Jesus wanted it to be. We can certainly see each of these various types of churches in New England!

Jesus' warnings and the promises he gives provide answers to how revitalization in a local church can occur. There was something about who Jesus is and about what Jesus said that each church was failing to believe and live out. Jesus frames his words in light of each church's local, physical and historical context.

The individual problems of each of the seven churches can be summarized as follows:

- Ephesus was a "Loveless" church, excelling in truth but lacking in love.
- Smyrna was a "Vulnerable" church, contemplating quitting in the face of hardship.
- Pergamum was a "Drifting" church who was misusing the word of God.
- Thyatira was a "Confused" church with competing authorities on how to interpret the Scriptures.
- Sardis was a "Nostalgic" church, unaware of their present spiritual decline and vulnerability.
- Philadelphia was a "Non-Missional" church, no longer moving forward on mission.
- Laodicea was a "Worldly" church, that looked more like the world than Christ.

The objective in identifying the church types is not to box a church into a particular category. Rather, the goal is to help God's people humble themselves, accurately assess themselves and to pray specifically for one another. God desires every church to thrive. For that to happen, a church must know its starting point as well as the next steps.

The better one understands a church the more specifically one can pray for it. For each of the seven churches, their specific prayer needs will be broken down into the following general categories:

- Strengths to be thankful for
- Weaknesses that need addressed
- Specific actions to pray for
- Knowing Jesus better
- Promise for the church to believe
- Specific needs of the leadership

Each chapter about a specific church will end with a prayer chart that can be used to help you pray specifically for that type of church.

My ministry context is New England. There are thousands of unhealthy churches in these six states that are on the downward decline, and without successful intervention, they will likely die. Each of these churches mirrors one of the seven types of churches we find in Revelation. They need us to pray for them.

Sadly, many of these churches are the only gospel witnesses left in their communities. New England communities, like all communities, desperately needs the remaining churches to fulfill their mission. When churches are not healthy, the entire community suffers. Overseed was founded in 2008 to help address this need for church revitalization in New England.

Overseed coaches Revitalization pastors and church leaders in New England in the dynamics of biblical church revitalization so they can successfully lead their churches to a healthy state. We believe God loves and desires each declining New England church to be healthy again; to re-embrace the gospel, to love each other, and to live on mission reaching their community for Christ.

Church revitalization is a challenging undertaking. I have written previously on the process of replanting/revitalizing a church in *Church Replanter: Learning from Nehemiah's example of leading change when things are really broken.* I would also recommend my colleague Jack L. Daniel's book *Patient Catalyst: Leading Church Revitalization.*

The journey for a church to flourish once again begins with prayer. So again, how do we best pray for churches in need of revitalization? We need to pray for churches to live out all the doctrines and commands of scripture. We also need to pray specifically for the individual situation of each church. Jesus' words to the seven churches in Asia Minor give us a model for how to pray contextually for the various types of churches needing revitalization.

Let us begin our journey with the "Loveless" church at Ephesus.

4 | Loveless Churches (Ephesus)

4 | Loveless Churches (Ephesus)

Truth is important. Discerning what is true from what is false is necessary for life. Jesus wanted people to understand the truth. He wanted them to know what the Scriptures actually taught and what they did not teach, the difference between true and false doctrine.

Jesus did not shrink from confronting the Jewish teachers of his day about their theological errors. In one instance, Jesus challenged the religious leaders about how they had missed the overarching story of the Scriptures. Despite knowing the Scriptures well, they had missed understanding Jesus was the Messiah. They knew the facts of the Scriptures, but it was not life-giving to them. Truth is important, yet truth alone can become sterile.

For the church at Ephesus, truth was a big deal. To understand the church's heavy emphasis on truth, it is necessary to understand some things about this church's early beginnings.

The city of Ephesus was the capital of the Roman province of Asia Minor. It was a major commercial port located at the mouth of the Cayster River on the Aegean coast. Today, this would be in the southwestern corner of Turkey. It was the third largest city in the Roman empire with an estimated population of 250,000 people.[40]

---

[40] David Seal, "Ephesus," *The Lexham Bible Dictionary.*

Ephesus was known for the Artemis shrine,[41] which provided the area with a lucrative tourist business from pilgrims traveling to Ephesus to visit the temple. The temple also served as a financial institution. The wealthy in Ephesus deposited money with the temple for which they were paid interest. The temple would then lend out that money to others like a local bank.[42]

Beginning in Acts 18, Luke shares how the church at Ephesus was founded on the ministries of Paul, Priscilla and Aquila, and Apollos. Paul had recently planted the church at Corinth. He, along with Priscilla and Aquila, were journeying back to his sending church in Antioch to report on what God had done during his second missionary journey. Their return trip brought them through Ephesus.

They came to Ephesus and Paul began sharing the gospel in the Synagogue. The Jews in Ephesus were interested in the gospel message. They asked Paul to stay longer, but he was unable because of his need to get back to Antioch. He did, however, leave his two ministry partners, Priscilla and Aquila, there to continue to minister to this small but growing church.

After this, a Jew named Apollos came to Ephesus. He was a great speaker and he loved to teach about Jesus. However, Apollos did not have the whole theological picture correct,

---

[41] The Artemis shrine was considered one of the seven wonders of the world.
[42] David Seal, "Ephesus," *The Lexham Bible Dictionary.*

knowing only the baptism of John. Priscilla and Aquila took him aside and mentored him more fully in understanding what the scriptures taught about Jesus. Apollos ministered at Corinth and then moved on to Achaia.

Paul, after updating his sending church at Antioch on the results of his ministry in Asia Minor, returned to Ephesus. He found upon his return some disciples, who, like Apollos, had only known the baptism of John. Paul instructed them further about Jesus, correcting their theological misunderstanding of John's message.

Paul spent the next two years boldly reasoning and persuading the residents of Ephesus and all of Asia Minor about the kingdom of God. Paul's message was confirmed by many miracles including the casting out of demons. Paul's ministry was so effective that some Jewish exorcists tried to incorporate Paul's methods.

> Then some of the itinerant Jewish exorcists undertook to invoke the name of the Lord Jesus over those who had evil spirits, saying, "I adjure you by the Jesus whom Paul proclaims." Seven sons of a Jewish high priest named Sceva were doing this. But the evil spirit answered them, "Jesus I know, and Paul I recognize, but who are you?" And the man in whom was the evil spirit leaped on them, mastered all of them and overpowered them, so that they fled out of that house naked and wounded.[43]

---

[43] Acts 19:13–16

Again, the church in Ephesus experienced well-meaning people attempting to minister, but out of a position of theological error.

As Paul's ministry flourished, it began impacting the income of those owning businesses focused on the magic arts and the worship of Artemis. [44] People had stopped spending money on books and shrines as they turned from worshipping false gods to Jesus Christ. Irritated business owners began to fight back, asserting their own counter theological positions and applying political pressure on Christians.

Right from the start, theological error was a challenge for the church in Ephesus. Paul, along with Priscilla and Aquila, had to contend with a truncated view of the Gospel within the church as well as opposition to the Gospel from outside the church.

Now, some forty year later, Jesus has these words for the church in Ephesus in Revelation 2:1-7:

> "To the angel of the church in Ephesus write: 'The words of him who holds the seven stars in his right hand, who walks among the seven golden lampstands. " 'I know your works,

---

[44] Artemis, was the Greek name of Diana, the goddess of hunting. She was the twin sister of Apollo. Her temple at Ephesus was one of the seven wonders of the world. She was worshiped as the "virgin goddess" and was considered as a mother goddess of Asia Minor. Her temple was supported on one hundred massive columns. Tradition claims that her image fell there from the sky (Acts 19:35) and is thought to refer to a meteorite. Her silversmiths made good money by making small pottery shrines. Spiros Zodhiates, *The Complete Word Study Dictionary: New Testament.*

your toil and your patient endurance, and how you cannot bear with those who are evil, but have tested those who call themselves apostles and are not, and found them to be false. I know you are enduring patiently and bearing up for my name's sake, and you have not grown weary.

But I have this against you, that you have abandoned the love you had at first. Remember therefore from where you have fallen; repent, and do the works you did at first. If not, I will come to you and remove your lampstand from its place, unless you repent.

Yet this you have: you hate the works of the Nicolaitans, which I also hate. He who has an ear, let him hear what the Spirit says to the churches. To the one who conquers I will grant to eat of the tree of life, which is in the paradise of God.'

Jesus, the one speaking, is the supreme authority over all creation as designated by the description of him holding the seven stars in his hand. This is probably a reference to a coin that the Emperor Domitian had minted in memory of his son who had died. The inscription read: "the divine Caesar, son of the emperor Domitian." The coin had seven stars which encircled the image of the son as he sat upon a globe. Thus, Jesus proclaims that His authority, rather than the Emperor's, is of ultimate cosmic significance.[45]

---

[45] Jim MacGregor, *Jesus' Words to Seven Churches of Roman Asia*, p. 63

Jesus commends the church for both its toil and perseverance. There was an active and passive side to their commendable lifestyle. They had worked hard at laboring for the Gospel. They had also endured the opposition of a society at odds with the church's goals and efforts.

To their credit, the church had continued to oppose theological error. They worked hard at discerning the theological truth of both visiting teachers and those who were a part of the local church. They had taken Paul's final warning to the Ephesians elders to heart and how they needed to be on guard testing what was taught by the Scriptures, and to expect that

> after my departure fierce wolves will come in among you, not sparing the flock; [46]

In the early church there were traveling leaders/teachers, also called apostles, who visited the churches. When the traveling teachers came to Ephesus, the church responded by faithfully testing their teachings against Scripture and discerning any falsehood. They had grown skillful in sniffing out theological error, never tiring of fighting for the purity of the Gospel. Jesus praises them for their intolerance of theological false teaching and testing teachers according to God's word.[47]

---

[46] Acts 20:29
[47] 2 John 9-10

The church had no patience for liberal theological thinking either. They hated the deeds of the Nicolaitans. They knew that belief and behavior mattered. Something the people of God are not always good at. Throughout the Bible, we find examples of the people of God ignoring God's clear requirement for personal holiness. At times it got so bad, the priests actually taught that personal holiness did not even matter.[48]

While the exact identity of the Nicolaitans remains unknown, they were probably an early Christian sect that advocated accommodation with pagan religions. Jesus refers, later in Revelation 2, to Balaam and Jezebel, two key Old Testament figures associated with the worship of pagan gods and immorality.[49] This would indicate that Jesus' commendation of the Ephesian Church is for its continued opposition of idolatry and accommodation to cultural norms. [50]

Jesus commends them for taking His word seriously. Yet, Jesus did have a serious problem with the church. They had left their first love. Their affections were no longer moved by their relationship with Jesus Christ. They were responding to the truth with conviction, humility, and concern but they were no

---

48 Ezekiel 22:26
49 Numbers 31:16; 1 Kings 18:19
50 Beale, *Revelation*, 249.

longer calmed, comforted, excited, or filled with uncontainable joy.[51]

They were unmoved relationally in their hearts. Jesus does not want to be known and understood like an animal in an experiment. Rather, the believer's experience of Christ should mirror Peter's description:

> Though you have not seen him, you love him. Though you do not now see him, you believe in him and rejoice with joy that is inexpressible and filled with glory,[52]

Yes, "orthodoxy is important, but orthodoxy alone will not do."[53] The strength of their head had dulled their heart. They were not shifting theologically, but they were drifting relationally. Their focus on sound doctrine and rooting out all imposters had the unintended consequence of creating a climate of suspicion in which brotherly love could no longer exist and cooled theirs hearts toward God.[54]

Their good actions were no longer fueled by a love for Jesus and each other. They had drifted in the same direction as the Pharisees, whom Jesus rebuked.

---

[51] Keller, *Prayer*, 159
[52] 1 Peter 1:8
[53] Seiss, *Lectures on the Apocalypse*, Vol 1, 165.
[54] Mounce, *The Book of Revelation*, 88.

> You search the Scriptures because you think that in them you
> have eternal life; and it is they that bear witness about me, yet
> you refuse to come to me that you may have life.[55]

Their love for Jesus was growing cold. When love declines, the soul loses its anchor and begins to drift. This loss of love for Jesus by the Ephesian church was a most serious condition. Christ alone is worthy of love. For in Christ alone is found the fullest satisfaction for the soul.[56]

Thomas Kempis frames this so well:

> Through humility you will show me what I am, what I have
> been, and from whence I came, for I am nothing, and did not
> know. If I'm left to myself, then I am nothing and all is frailty
> and imperfection; but if you vouchsafe a little regard to me,
> soon I have made strong, and filled with a new joy. ... I have
> lost you, and myself as well, by the inordinate love I have had
> for myself; in seeking you again I have found both you and
> myself. Therefore, I will from now on more deeply set myself
> as naught and more diligently seek you that I have done in
> past times.[57]

Without love, there is a growing crack in the very foundation of a Christian's character. For love. as Paul tell us, is what makes service and the use of spiritual gifts valuable. For without love, they are worthless. Without love, the church's words are

---

[55] John 5:39–40
[56] Ford C. Otttman, *The Unfolding of the Ages*, 30.
[57] Thomas a Kempis, *The Imitation of Christ*, 117.

nothing but a noisy gong and a clanging cymbal. Even if they knew all mysteries and had all knowledge, without love they would be nothing.[58] The church's witness must flow from a love for God.

Often, throughout church history, those churches that are strongest in biblical orthodoxy tend to become relationally cold. Correctness can be a great motivator. However, accuracy alone can easily lead to a truncated gospel, especially in subsequent generations. Barclay comments how

> the eagerness to root out all mistaken men had ended in a sour and rigid orthodoxy.

Using knowledge to enforce behavior has been an Achilles heel for the church throughout the generations. Tom Holland, in his book *Dominion,* describes this same problem in the Church in 1200 A.D.

> As never before, the ambition of the Church to provide a salvation to peoples of every race and background had become a weapon to be turned against all who spurned its offer.[59]

Without love, the gospel message easily becomes weaponized for selfish preference and ambition. The call to the believer is clear – love God with all your heart, soul, mind, and strength, and each other as yourselves. Christianity is relational at its

---

[58] 1 Corinthians 13:1-3
[59] Tom Holland, *Dominion,* Kindle Locations 4271-4272.

core. God walked with Adam in the cool of the evening and God desires the same walk with his children today. The believer should resonate with the song, "If ever I loved The, my Jesus, 'tis now."[60]

Jesus, when he addresses the church at Ephesus, describes Himself as the One

> who holds the seven stars in his right hand, who walks among the seven golden lampstands. [61]

Jesus has all the authority in the universe, and He uses His authority to walk with his brothers and sisters in deep relationship. Jesus wants to relate to us as friends, not as forced slaves. Jesus called the apostles his friends and gave them His joy.

When the Ephesian church was planted, they loved Jesus. He was the new center of their entire world. They had a passion for Jesus and His word. They desired to know God. They searched out the truth of God's word. Their ministry affected much of Asia Minor.

Yet, somewhere along the way they lost their first love. Knowing about Jesus took preference over really knowing

---

[60] William R. Featherston, *My Jesus, I Love Thee.*
[61] Revelation 2:1

Jesus. Talking about Jesus replaced the desire to talk with Jesus. Theology overshadowed mission.

It did not happen all once. Rather, there were subtle shifts over the course of their forty-year history. They slowly drifted apart from their relationship with Jesus. It's similar to what can happen in any marriage.

Jesus encourages the church to

> Remember, therefore, from where you have fallen; repent, and do the works you did at first. If not, I will come to you and remove your lampstand from its place, unless you repent.[62]

The way forward begins with remembering. The church needs to reconnect with Jesus by repenting and doing the deeds it did at first. The "deeds," or as it is often translated "works," denote comprehensively both what a man is and how he acts.[63] Jesus is calling them back to a loving relationship with Himself, and out of the overflow of that love, to the mission of sharing Christ in their community.

Jesus taught that out the of the abundance of the heart a man speaks. The book of James shows how true faith results in godly and loving behavior. The Ephesian church needed to

---

[62] Revelation 2:5

[63] Spiros Zodhiates, *The Complete Word Study Dictionary: New Testament.*

reconnect relationally with Jesus and move out on mission, a mission that is motivated by love once again.

The Ephesian church had persevered despite opposition to the Gospel by those outside the church. They had willingly paid the price relationally and economically to follow Christ.

Jesus concludes His message to the Ephesian church by encouraging them to overcome, to hold fast to the truth of the Scriptures. If they do, He extends the promise of eating from the tree of life in Paradise. This would be something far better than the rich food served at the city's idolatrous and licentious festivals they were missing out on.[64] Instead, they can look forward to experiencing the reality depicted in Revelation 22. They will live in the new Jerusalem with Christ.

Despite the glorious future that awaits them, the threat of persecution has dampened their enthusiasm for evangelism. Jesus exhorts them to not lose sight of the mission. They can conquer and overcome their fears.

So how ought we pray for a church like Ephesus? I can personally identify the church at Ephesus. My own personal tendency is to lean into my "word" gift. To love truth. I greatly enjoy learning about Jesus and the Scriptures. Yet, I must be

---

[64] Hendrickson, *More than Conquerors,* 63.

sensitive to also discern whether or not I feel connected to Jesus. Do I love the savior I enjoy learning about?

So how do we pray for a loveless church like Ephesus? A church that is truth-oriented, but whose members have grown cold towards Jesus. The scriptural model is to begin praying with thanksgiving. We see this in many of Paul's prayers for the churches. So, I encourage you to also begin praying for a church like Ephesus with thanksgiving.

There is much to be thankful for in a church that resembles Ephesus. Their grasp of theology is an important contribution to the larger church. Their willingness to call out false teachers and to confront sin is a blessing. Their hard work and endurance set an example for other churches. We should thank God for these qualities.

Next, ask God to open the eyes of churches like this to once again see Jesus. Ask the Holy Spirit to bring to their remembrance how their relationship with Jesus used to be. Ask that these believers would see from where they have fallen, to repent and reconnect relationally with Jesus; to both embrace and to live out all that the Bible teaches.[65]

Pray for the church to get back to the basics of mission and ministry. Jesus' mission for each church is to make disciples;

---

[65] John 14:21

disciples who know the word, obey the word, and are themselves on the same mission.

Ask God to give the church wisdom to frame its ministry relationally rather than solely theologically. For the church to have the wisdom to aim its teaching at both the head and the heart. For the church to motivate people to love Jesus not merely think correctly about Jesus. Ask God that the church's disciple-making efforts would move God's people to love Him with all their heart, soul, mind, and strength.

Pray for their works to flow from a heart of loving devotion to Jesus. Unfortunately, there are such things as "dead works," those works which have no life-connection with piety. They are works put on from without, and not brought forth from within. These works are like fruit tied upon the tree, not the product of a life of faith.[66]

Ask God to graciously grant this type of church to love Jesus. That they would

> Set their hearts on fire to love you, oh Christ our Lord, that in its flame they made love you with all their heart, mind, soul, and strengthen and love their neighbor as themselves, so that, keeping your commandments, they may glorify you, the giver of all good gifts.[67]

---

[66] Seiss, *Lectures on the Apocalypse,* Vol1, 166.
[67] Eastern Orthodox Prayer, 5th Century.

The reward to loving Jesus is very great. Jesus promises,

> To the one who conquers I will grant to eat of the tree of life, which is in the paradise of God.[68]

Father, we pray that you might warm the hearts of your people in churches like in Ephesus, and for your people to encounter You afresh with tender hearts. We ask that they would be more amazed at who You are, than at the theological constructs of your wisdom revealed in the Scriptures. May you grant the great truths of orthodoxy to soften their hearts, to move them to repentance and to a deepening heartfelt friendship with Jesus for all eternity. We pray for hearts of love that overflow in ministry to the community.

In addition to praying through the Scriptures for this type of church, you can use the prayer chart below for ideas on how to pray:

---

[68] Revelation 2:7

Praying for Loveless Churches like Ephesus

Observations	Prayer Ideas
Strengths to be thankful for	• Their ability to discern truth. • Their desire for the purity of the church. • Their hard-working approach to ministry. • Their patient endurance.
Weakness that needs addressed	• To realize they have abandoned Jesus, their first love. • To not love truth at the expense of a heart that loves people. • To not beat people with the truth, but to lovingly live on mission.
Specific actions to pray for	• To encounter Jesus, the true authority. • To repent of their lack of love for God and each other. • For the gospel truth to melt their hearts. • To see and implement ways to love, and to serve their community. • To hear what the Spirit is saying about ways to move forward with mission.

	• To overcome by faith and experience God's salvific presence
Knowing Jesus better, to see Jesus	• As present in their midst. • As wanting to engage them relationally. • As the one to be loved above all else.
Promise for the church to believe	• To be able experience the life-giving presence of God (Tree of life).
For the Leadership	• To demonstrate how to live a loving life.

5 | Vulnerable Churches (Smyrna)

5 | Vulnerable Churches (Smyrna)

Jesus' own ministry demonstrated that the way forward in ministry is not by power but weakness. Jesus rebukes Peter for fighting back with a sword at His arrest, explaining how he could ask the Father and receive 12 legions of angels to fight for him. In the snap of a finger there could have been 96,000 angels defending Him.[69] However, Jesus said no to power. From the moment of Jesus' birth, his method was to always reject power as the means to force the ministry forward.

So how can the Church function in this world when it is vulnerable? Can the Church survive and even thrive in a world dominated by power? Jesus speaks to this very issue in His message to the vulnerable church at Smyrna.

Smyrna was an ancient city located on the west coast of Asia Minor. It was situated at the head of the gulf into which flows the Hermus River. The city was located 40 miles north of Ephesus which is now the present-day Turkish city of Izmir.[70]

Smyrna was one of the seven postal districts, which made up the most crucial part of the Roman province of Asia Minor.[71] It is likely that Paul or one of his companions introduced Christianity to Smyrna.[72]

Smyrna was an important seaport in Asia Minor due to its location on the edge of the trade route into the region. Smyrna

---

69 Matthew 26:52-53
70 David Seal, "Smyrna," *The Lexham Bible Dictionary.*
71 J. Massyngberde Ford, *Revelation.*
72 See Acts 19:9–10, 26

was famous for its beauty, wealth, and fine wines. The city excelled in medicine and science.[73] It was home to various trade guilds for fishermen, tanners, silversmiths, and goldsmiths.[74]

The residents of Smyrna were particularly loyal to Rome and its emperor worship. Thus, political and business success were directly tied to civic engagement and the worship of Caesar. This caused a conflict for Christians. For example, membership in the trade guilds required sacrificing both to a local pagan deity and to the emperor.[75] Thus, for believers who refused to engage in the worship of anyone other than Jesus, their access to economic and social wealth was restricted.

The church in Smyrna is only mentioned in the Bible in Revelation two. Jesus sent these words to the church at Smyrna in Revelation 2:8-11:

> "And to the angel of the church in Smyrna write: 'The words of the first and the last, who died and came to life. I know your tribulation and your poverty (but you are rich) and the slander of those who say that they are Jews and are not, but are a synagogue of Satan.
>
> Do not fear what you are about to suffer. Behold, the devil is about to throw some of you into prison, that you may be tested, and for ten days you will have tribulation. Be faithful unto

---

73 Strabo, *Geography* 14.1.15, 12.8.20.
74 Harland, *Sphere of Contention*, 55.
75 Kraybill, *Imperial Cult*, 196.

death, and I will give you the crown of life. He who has an ear, let him hear what the Spirit says to the churches. The one who conquers will not be hurt by the second death.' "

The city of Smyrna was affluent, yet those in the church were not. Jesus reminds them that though they were economically poor, the good news was that they were spiritually wealthy. They were rich in the things that mattered for eternity. In Ephesians 1, the apostle Paul lays out in detail how spiritual rich believers are in this world, and even more in the next. Paul concludes with these words:

> *I pray that* having the eyes of your hearts enlightened, that you may know what is the hope to which he has called you, what are the riches of his glorious inheritance in the saints, and what is the immeasurable greatness of his power toward us who believe, according to the working of his great might.[76]

Yet, those in the church in Smyrna wrestled with how to deal with their own present-day realities. These believers were very susceptible to being persecuted and misunderstood since they were without wealth, status, or influence. They had few civic options for protecting themselves from this persecution.

In addition, the church also faced the slander of the Jews directed toward them.[77] This slander, emanating from the

---

[76] Ephesians 1:18–19
[77] John labels the Jews here as not real Jews. He is speaking spiritually not addressing national descent, as Paul does in Roman 2:28-29.

synagogue, was fueled by a false gospel that vilified Jesus and demanded adherence to the Old Testament law.[78]

Some of the Jews in Smyrna and in other cities of Asia Minor were collaborating with city officials against Christians. There is evidence that Jews in Smyrna participated wholeheartedly in the infamous martyrdom of Polycarp, which would occur in the next century.[79]

Christians were easy targets because of their singular loyalty to Jesus. Anyone refusing to sacrifice to the emperor would be seen as politically disloyal. They could be arrested and severely punished under Roman law.

Jesus warns the church that the worst was yet to come. They were about to experience intense suffering. Some of them were going to be cast into prison, tried, and executed. This was in addition to being poverty-stricken, often caused after losing their jobs due to their conversion to Christ.[80]

Jesus encourages them to not be deceived by false hope nor to be afraid. Jesus is clear, He was not going to use His immense power to prevent the suffering from coming. They would have to go through it. However, Jesus would make His power available to them to enable them to persevere through the coming suffering.

---

[78] The council at Jerusalem in Acts 15 and the letter to the Galatians addresses the Jewish confusion over what the scriptures teach.
[79] *Martyrdom of Polycarp,* 13.1, 17.2
[80] Hendrickson, *More than Conquerors,* 64-65.

Yes, suffering is coming, but the good news is that it will not be endless. There will be ten days of tribulation. A reference to Daniel and his three friends who were also tested for 10 days, after being unwilling to compromise their faith by honoring the King above God. Similarly, in Smyrna, there will be a beginning and an end to the suffering. Their challenge was to remain faithful to Jesus throughout the testing, even if it meant death.

Jesus describes Himself as "the first and the last, who was dead, and has come to life." Jesus is the conqueror of death. It is Jesus, the resurrected King, who promises to give them the crown of life. By remaining faithful, they are promised participation in Christ's heavenly victorious rule.

They were facing earthly tribulation and defeat. It was critical that they anchor their hope in the promised eternal victory and blessing to come. Yes, some of them would suffer an earthly martyrdom. However, they could be assured that those who did suffer martyrdom would not be hurt by the second death. They could expect eternal life!

Often, the church can find itself vulnerable, from a worldly perspective. Oddly, this is good since Jesus' power is made perfect in weakness.[81] Dependence is to be the normal state of the believer. Helplessness should move the church to prayer. Paul encourages the Philippian church:

> Do not be anxious about anything, but in everything by
> prayer and supplication with thanksgiving let your requests

---

[81] 2 Corinthians 12:9

be made known to God. And the peace of God, which surpasses all understanding, will guard your hearts and your minds in Christ Jesus. [82]

Unfortunately, the church, rather than embracing her weakness, often seeks a different solution to avoid being vulnerable. As was mentioned when describing the church at Ephesus, the church is often tempted to pursue a "will to power."[83] The church attempts to rid herself of weakness by seizing power to dominate, control or rule the world.[84]

God's call is contrary to any such thinking. His call is a call to the weakness of the cross. The Scriptures teach that weakness is good. God chooses the weak of this world to put to shame the strong in order to bring more glory to Himself.[85] We are to embrace our weakness by embracing God's power. We do not need more strength. Rather, we need to humble ourselves and ask God to use His unlimited power to move the Kingdom forward.

Rather than embracing power, the scriptures advocate being a faithful witness to the Gospel. For the Gospel is the power of God for salvation.[86] Jesus' encouragement to the church at Smyrna was to remain faithful in the present, despite their vulnerability.

---

[82] Philippians 4:6–7
[83] A concept that flows from the writings of Nietzsche.
[84] Hunter, *How To Change The World*, p 103-106
[85] 1 Cor 1: 26-31
[86] Romans 1:16

The church needs grace to persevere despite her weakness. She needs grace to remain steadfast to Jesus' calling. She needs to ask God to

> Give me grace, oh God, to hear you calling and to follow your guiding ... You offer us yourself and all your goods. Give us grace to receive them. You show us the way to irreplaceable benefits; enable us not to turn aside, until we have taken possession of them.
>
> Give us consistency and steadiness of purpose, that our thoughts may not be fleeting, fickle, and ineffectual, but that we may perform all things within an immovable mind to the glory of your holy name. Through Christ our Lord.[87]

The present circumstances are not the whole story. There is a cosmic battle going on and the Church's real enemy is Satan. As Paul taught, the Church is wrestling

> not against flesh and blood, but against the rulers, against the authorities, against the cosmic powers over this present darkness, against the spiritual forces of evil in the heavenly places.[88]

So how should we pray for a church like Smyrna, a church that is vulnerable both politically and economically, and has been marginalized by her local community?

---

[87] Ludovicus Vives quoted in George Appleton, ed. *The Oxford Book of Prayer*, 117-118.
[88] Ephesians 6:12

Again, we start by thanking God for churches that resemble Smyrna. This church has remained spiritually strong despite her circumstances and what she is facing. The church has not given up. There are many churches in New England that from a human point of view should have shut their doors a long time ago. Yet, they refuse to give up.[89] Praise God!

We need to pray for those in a church resembling Smyrna to hold onto the reality that Jesus knows their humble state and their present tribulation. Jesus is not far off. He walks among them. He knows what they are going through.

Their humble state does not mean Jesus sees them as unimportant. Jesus has not abandoned them for people with better positions in society or those with greater wealth or earthly influence.

Pray that the church would find strength in its union and communion with Christ.[90] For them to experience the reality of what J.I.Packer wrote:

> Prayer is a means to energy. Spiritual alertness, vigor, and confidence are the regular spin-off from earnest prayer.[91]

We need to pray for the church to reject looking for ways to hijack the world's power as the answer to their vulnerability.

---

[89] Some might argue that it would be best if these churches had died. Such a view misses the heart of God throughout the OT who delighted to renew the people of Israel over and over again. These churches need revitalized, new leadership and renewed gospel preaching. Thus, a book on praying for these churches.

[90] John 15:1ff

[91] Packer, *Knowing Christianity*, 128.

Instead, for them to seek God and His power, to find, as Paul did, that God's power is made perfect in weakness. Ask God to give them the grace to be able to say with Paul:

> For this light momentary affliction is preparing for us an eternal weight of glory beyond all comparison, as we look not to the things that are seen but to the things that are unseen. For the things that are seen are transient, but the things that are unseen are eternal.[92]

We also need to pray for this type of church to match their orthodox belief with genuine Christian conduct. Their problem was one of poor application. The church needs to be able to see life as an integrated spiritual plane. They needed to choose to behave in the present in the light of eternity.

Their battle is a spiritual one with real world implications. Much like the promise of Jesus in Revelation, James also encourages the church:

> Blessed is the man who remains steadfast under trial, for when he has stood the test he will receive the crown of life, which God has promised to those who love him.[93]

The enemy's goal is to make them compromise their faith. Satan wants them to abandon their sole allegiance to Jesus. He wants them to be ok with living a life disconnected from what they believe, to blend in with the local culture and the Roman worldview.

---

[92] 2 Corinthians 4:17–18
[93] James 1:12

We need to pray for the believers in this type of church to reject Satan's plan. For them to serve the Lord Jesus Christ with a singular focus of Daniel. That they would refuse to compromise, even if that results in capital punishment.

We need to pray for the church to persevere. Ask God to fulfill his promise to preserve these faithful saints.[94] For them to continue to trust Christ and His promises despite the current circumstances. For them to be courageous in God's strength despite their own weakness and to live out of the resources of Christ rather than focusing on their own vulnerability.

Often these churches, at least in America in the early twenty-first century, are full of older saints who are tired and often fearful. Ask God to give them the wisdom to leverage the Kingdom resources God has given them. They have a building plus decades or centuries of history within the community to build upon.

We need to ask God to also provide economically for these types of churches. These churches do not consist of the well-to-do, but rather everyday folk who have been faithfully committed to the church over many years. It is often an aging congregation with limited resources.

We must pray for the church to hear what the Holy Spirit is saying to them. For the church to be able to maintain a non-anxious presence as it lives for eternity rather than for earthly

---

94 Psalm 31:23

comfort and safety. For them to engage in the mission of the local church once again.

Father, we ask You to empower your people in churches like the one in Smyrna. For them to not give in to despair, but to face the difficulty of their life with courage flowing from faith in you. May your disciples find Your promise of eternal life to be the ground of their perseverance as they engage the difficulties of day-to-day life. For them to embrace a lifestyle of taking up their cross daily and following Jesus on mission to their community. For their hearts to be convinced of the truth that following Jesus is worth the cost.

In addition to your prayers that flow from the commands and doctrines of scripture, you can use the prayer chart below for ideas on how to pray for this type of church:

Praying for Vulnerable Churches like Smyrna	
Observations	Prayer Ideas
Strengths to be thankful for	• They have not quit. • They are rich spiritually because they are believers.

Weakness that needs addressed	• To not feel abandoned by God even though they are vulnerable. • To not be afraid of suffering. • To have an eternal perspective, they will not be hurt by the second death.
Specific actions to pray for	• To remember Jesus knows them. • To live from the perspective that they are rich in Christ. • To integrate how they live with what they believe and to see the current disconnects. • To make decisions with gospel intentionality, looking at the rewards in the next life • To embrace ministry, and to engage their community with the Gospel. • For God to preserve them and for the Kingdom to not lose their facilities. • For God to provide for them economically. • To keep the biblical perspective that all suffering has an end point. For them to live for eternity. • To conquer by faith knowing the promise of eternity with Jesus awaits them.

Knowing Jesus better, to see Jesus	• As the powerful resurrected savior. • As the eternal one. • As divinely sovereign over history.
Promise for the church to believe	• To not live out of fear, but rather by faith because Jesus will give them eternal life.
For Leadership	• To demonstrate how to live a life of faith.

6 | Drifting Churches (Pergamum)

6 | Drifting Church (Pergamum)

Central to the life of the Church is faith. Faith fuels the Church's worship and mission. The Christian life flows from knowing and relating to her Savior, Jesus Christ. Yet, what if the message of Jesus got distorted? Imagine what the impact on the church would be if their faith was compromised by believing in a distorted gospel?

Jesus speaks to the church at Pergamum by highlighting that he knows where they live. They live where Satan's throne resides. This is probably a reference to fact that Pergamum was the capital of the province and, therefore, the center of emperor-worship.[95] Thus, growing tension existed between the teachings of the imperial cult and Christian beliefs.

Like the other churches in this region, the Gospel probably reached Pergamum during Paul's third missionary journey as he resided in Ephesus.[96]

As with some of the other seven churches, the assembly in Pergamum is only mentioned in the Bible in Revelation two. Jesus sends these words to the church at Pergamum in Revelation 2:12-17:

> "And to the angel of the church in Pergamum write: 'The words of him who has the sharp two-edged sword. I know where you

---

[95] Hendrickson, *More than Conquerors,* 66.
[96] Acts 19:10.

dwell, where Satan's throne is. Yet you hold fast my name, and you did not deny my faith even in the days of Antipas my faithful witness, who was killed among you, where Satan dwells.

But I have a few things against you: you have some there who hold the teaching of Balaam, who taught Balak to put a stumbling block before the sons of Israel, so that they might eat food sacrificed to idols and practice sexual immorality. So also you have some who hold the teaching of the Nicolaitans.

Therefore repent. If not, I will come to you soon and war against them with the sword of my mouth. He who has an ear, let him hear what the Spirit says to the churches. To the one who conquers I will give some of the hidden manna, and I will give him a white stone, with a new name written on the stone that no one knows except the one who receives it.' "

Pergamum, present day Bergama in Turkey, was the center of both the Roman government and the pagan cult of emperor worship. It was also the center of many other pagan cults in Asia Minor with their various deities. There was a striking conical hill behind Pergamum. On this prominent hill were many large and beautiful temples dedicated to these various gods.

Jesus, in this message to Pergamum, identifies Satan as the one behind this pluralistic menagerie of false gods. While on earth, Jesus taught that Satan was a thief who came only to steal, kill, and destroy.[97] Satan's primary strategy for centuries was to blind people to the true God by offering them an array of false gods to worship instead.

Beginning with Pentecost, Satan's tactics have been centered around opposing and destroying the church. Satan's plan was the same in Pergamum, to oppose the church and its gospel message.

The city was especially proud of its dedication to Caesar worship. It was the first city in Asia Minor to build a temple to a Roman ruler. The city was known as the "Temple Warden." This was a rank or honor granted by the Roman Senate and the Emperor to certain cities which had built temples to the Emperor or had established cults to members of the Imperial family.[98]

Living in this politico-religious center would have put enormous pressure on a believer to pay homage to Caesar. For life in Pergamum was ordered around worshipping the Emperor. A refusal to participate in this worship of the Emperor would have meant high treason against the state.[99]

The realty of this conflict was fresh in their minds due to recent martyrdom of Antipas. Antipas was executed by the Romans for refusing to recant of his sole allegiance to

---

[97] John 10:10
[98] Chisholm, Hugh, ed., "Neocorate," Encyclopedia Britannica (11th ed.).
[99] Charles, Revelation I, 61 and Beale, The Book of Revelation, 246.

worshipping Jesus. This pressure to join the citizens of Pergamum in their syncretistic worship was literally a matter of life and death.

In most Greek cities, like Pergamum, the citizens were expected to sacrifice to the gods of that city's local religious tradition. They believed that these gods had shown the city favor in the past. If citizens refused to worship them it would anger the gods and cause them to withhold their favor. This worship was not just some theoretical concept. The life and health of the city was viewed as being dependent of the favor of these gods. The worship of these gods by all in the city, including Christians, would have been expected. It was a citizen's civic duty.

With the addition of emperor worship, refusing to worship was elevated to a crime against the state. Anyone refusing to worship the emperor could be consequently brought before the Roman authorities to give an account of their refusal. The authorities would then give them an opportunity to sacrifice to the emperor to prove their loyalty.[100] Antipas refused to compromise his faith by sacrificing to the emperor and he was executed.

Unlike Antipas, some in the church had chosen to compromise. They engaged in these non-Christian festivals along with the worship of false gods and the immoralities that characterized

---

[100] Beal, *The Book of Revelation*, 247

these feasts. To make matters worse, their actions were being supported by the false teaching that appeared in the church. Their compromised behavior was undermining their gospel witness to the community.

The elders of the church were adding to the confusion by neglecting to apply church discipline to the erring members promoting the false teachings and resulting sinful behavior. Thus, they were giving their unspoken approval of these unbiblical doctrines by refusing to confront them.

This is the opposite of the problem in Ephesus, where an overemphasis on internal doctrinal purity led to a lack of concern for the outside world. Here, de-emphasizing doctrinal purity led to the acceptance of false teaching and with it the resulting compromising behaviors. By allowing overidentification with the world, they weakened their witness to Jesus.

This false teaching took two forms. The first was to embrace a form of teaching similar to Balaam in the Old Testament. Balaam subtly put a stumbling block before Israel by encouraging them to embrace the worship of Baal, to eat the meat sacrificed in the context of this idolatrous worship and to commit acts of immorality.[101]

---

[101] Numbers 22-25, 31:16

Balaam knew that one way to seriously weaken Israel was the threat of syncretism. If Israel could be deceived into embracing other religious practices alongside with their worship of God, it would lead to the loss of their ethnic and religious identity. They would also consequently lose the blessing and promise of God.[102]

The practice of eating meat sacrificed to idols and committing sexual immorality were being defended by this false teaching. Even though these practices had been expressly forbidden by the apostles and elders of the early church.[103] This supposedly new teaching directly contradicted the Scriptures in the same manner as Balaam did, thousands of years previously.

These false teachers were arguing that believers were permitted to have a closer relationship with pagan culture, institutions, and religion.[104] They taught that it was permissible for Christians to engage in these secular/civic events, even though it meant celebrating the patron deities through sacrifices and the after parties focused on immorality.[105]

---

[102] David A. deSilva, "The Social Setting of the Revelation to John: Conflicts Within, Fears Without," 293.
[103] Acts 15:28-29
[104] Beale, *The Book of Revelation*, 248
[105] See Bruce Winter, *After Paul Left Corinth, The Influence of Secular, Ethics and Social Change.*

Their line of reasoning was probably similar to what Paul encountered in Corinth.[106] Their teaching went something like:

Afterall, Jesus knows these gods are nothing but false gods. So, why refuse to worship them and endure the resulting negative economic and social impact? Why risk your life when you could simply pay homage to a "make believe" God? Don't you know that refusing to participate could lead to you being brought before the authorities and executed, like Antipas? Also, if you don't participate, you'll lose all your friends. You will be cut off from much of the social life of the city.

The second form of compromise was embracing the teaching of the Nicolaitans. Not much is known definitively about these teachings.[107] Like Balaam, Nicolaitans were in some way advocating for a form of compromise with society. They taught something along the lines that personal holiness was neither a priority nor was it necessary. They advocated for the erroneous idea that behavior and belief can be safely separated. We do not know the exact doctrinal reasoning used

---

[106] Paul addressed similar thinking in Corinth, that "an idol is nothing," and therefore participation in an idol feast would have no spiritual significance. Since there was no denial of the gospel, nor affront to the lordship of Jesus, there was no reason for Christians to suffer economic hardship and even social ostracism. Accommodation, while keeping the teaching unharmed, was the best way forward for them to survive. David A. deSilva, "The Social Setting of the Revelation to John: Conflicts Within, Fears Without," 294.

[107] The church at Ephesus hated the deeds of Nicolaitans but here in Pergamum they embraced the teachings.

by the Nicolaitans, but this line of false thinking, called antinomianism, has been repeated throughout Church history, weakening and destroying many churches.

In Jesus' remarks to the church at Ephesus, the concern was over the *deeds* of the Nicolaitans. Here, the concern is over their *teachings*. Once sin enters the life of a church it is not long before sinners seek to justify their actions. They build up or adopt a false theology to soothe their guilty consciences.

They then leverage that teaching to get others to join them in their lifestyle, further soothing their consciences. The sad result is an unholy alliance with the world and a weakened witness to the Gospel of Jesus Christ.

The church in Pergamum needed to return to these opening lines of the Lord's prayer:

> Our Father in heaven, hallowed be your name. Your Kingdom come, your will be done, on earth as it is in heaven.[108]

Jesus is clear that the church at Pergamum needed to repent and re-engage with God's revealed will. Behavior and belief both matter. Believers are called to be holy as God is holy. If those at the church of Pergamum continue to embrace false teaching and engage in the disobedience those doctrines advocate, they will find themselves as the enemy of Jesus. He

---

[108] Matthew 6:9–10

will come and make war against them with the sword of His mouth.[109]

There is no denying that there is often a worldly cost to walking with Jesus. However, the church was failing to grasp that there was an even greater heavenly cost for compromising with the world.

Fortunately, if the church repents, their eternity is secure. Jesus assures them that though it will probably cost them a seat at the pagan feasts with all its delectable food, they are assured a seat at the heavenly marriage supper of Jesus where they will eat heavenly manna. They will receive a white stone identifying them as one of Christ's own, a VIP ticket to the feast.[110]

So how should we pray for a modern-day church like Pergamum, a church that is drifting theologically? A church where some have embraced teaching that is theologically wrong and contrary to the Gospel? A church that is misusing the sword the spirit, the word of God.

Again, we start by thanking God for a church that resembles Pergamum. Thankfully, this church continues to hold fast to

---

[109] Just as Balaam was killed by the sword for his refusal to repent. Numbers 22:23, 31, 31:8.

[110] White sones had two common associations. One was a vote of acquittal. The other was as a ticket for special occasions. Quite probably both associations were implied here. Beale, *The Book of Revelation*, 252-253. Also, see Beale's discussion on the "new name" 253-258.

Jesus in the face of very real persecution. This is a church that despite its theological compromise, will not deny Jesus.

This type of church's greatest need is to repent. They need to address their syncretism. On one hand, they do not deny Jesus and yet on the other hand they are denying the faith by embracing false teaching and its accompanying sinful behavior. We need to pray that God will open their eyes to this false understanding of what the Scriptures teach. Ask God to give them the grace to see their error and repent.

This is a church that has embraced teaching which focuses on grace at the expense of holiness. Living a life of holiness is hard. It is much easier to modify your doctrine than it is to change your lifestyle. The key prayer request for this church is for its members to reject this false teaching and turn away from participating in the worshipping of idols and sexual immorality.

Pray for them to embrace God's call to live a life of holiness, despite whatever it costs them.[111] A radical biblical holiness which begins with embracing the Bible and the lifestyle of holiness it teaches. Jesus taught that the pure in heart were blessed for they would see God.[112] Paul encouraged believers to keep themselves pure.[113] Biblical holiness is a doctrinal

---

[111] 1 Peter 1:14-16
[112] Matthew 5:8
[113] 1 Timothy 5:22

term deeply rooted in the Scriptures with a corresponding clear biblical definition. Christians are not free to change it.

Ask God to give the church the wisdom to think about behavior from an eternal perspective. Living holy often brings with it a present negative consequence. To choose to live holy is often simultaneously a choice to endure ill-treatment and to miss out on the passing pleasures of sin.[114] However, the Scriptures are clear that the future eternal reward promised by Jesus will far outweigh any present-day costs.

We need to pray for this type of church to regain a love for the Bible and to realign their theology with its teachings. Pray for them to move away from any creative but erroneous interpretations of the Scripture and return to orthodoxy.

Ask God to give those in the church the courage and fortitude to address their guilty consciences by repentance rather than by adjusting their theology. For the church to learn how to say "No!" to the lust of the flesh, the lust of the eyes and the boastful pride of life.[115]

Biblical theology and its resulting biblical holiness are not optional for the church. Pray for the church to embrace the authority of the Scriptures and to place themselves under the teaching of the Bible.

---

[114] Hebrews 11:24-26
[115] 1 John 2:15-16

The elders' primary responsibilities in addition to shepherding include doctrine, direction, and discipline. The elders at Pergamum were failing to fulfill their duties of following sound doctrine and consistent discipline. Ask God to give the elders of this type of church the courage and biblical insight to be faithful to their calling to apply church discipline to both those teaching false doctrine and those adopting the resulting sinful lifestyles. Pray for them not to allow false doctrine to enter into the fabric of church life.

Father, we pray for those who attend a church like the one at Pergamum. Give them the clarity to see and believe what your Scriptures teach. For them to be able to wade through false teaching and accurately handle the word of truth. For them not to give evil a foothold in their church. For hearts that desire to be holy as You are holy. For them to apply their creativity, not to doctrine, but to the gospel mission in their community.

In addition to your prayers that flow from the doctrines and commands of scripture, you can use the prayer chart below for ideas on how to pray for this type of church:

Praying for Drifting Churches like Pergamum

Observations	Prayer Ideas
Strengths to be thankful for	• They hold fast to Jesus' name. • They did not deny Jesus when the costs were high.

Weakness that needs addressed	• Embraced false teaching that allowed for participating in:
	  ◦ Idol worship
	  ◦ Sexual immorality
	• Elders failing to fulfill their duties.

Specific Actions to pray for	• Repentance of bad theology and wrong application of biblical doctrines. • Realignment of their theology with the Bible. • For elders to embrace their responsibility for doctrine, direction, and discipline. • To view cost and reward from an eternal perspective. • To overcome their sinful choices by faith.

Knowing Jesus better, to see Jesus	• As the one who gave the written word. • As the divine judge who will hold them accountable to His word.
Promise for the church to believe	• To long for fellowship in heaven with Christ as God's adopted sons and daughters.
For Leadership	• For God to open their eyes to the truth in God's word.

7 | Confused Churches (Thyatira)

7 | Confused Churches (Thyatira)

Once the church begins to embrace multiple sources of authority, confusion starts to set in. It becomes unclear who the member in the pew should trust. How is the church to move forward on mission when it is being asked to embrace competing truths?

Jesus now directs His words to the church at Thyatira. The city of Thyatira, today the town of Akhisar in western Turkey, was located on a branch of the Hermus River. Not much is known about the early history of the town.[116]

We are first introduced to Thyatira in Acts 16. The Holy Spirit had sent Paul to share the gospel in Macedonia, and the first city he came to was Philippi. He began proclaiming the Gospel, and his first convert to Christ was a woman named Lydia from the city of Thyatira.[117]

Lydia was known as a seller of purple fabrics. Her home city of Thyatira was famous for a special technology used in the dying of purple fabrics. They developed a dye that was uniquely made from the madder root rather than commonly used shellfish.[118] It is likely that Lydia maintained her connections

---

[116] R. North, "Thyatira," ed. Geoffrey W. Bromiley, *The International Standard Bible Encyclopedia, Revised* (Wm. B. Eerdmans, 1979–1988), 846.

[117] Acts 16:14

[118] A fact which Homer even references in his Iliad. Barrett, *A Critical and Exegetical Commentary on the Acts of the Apostles*, Vol 2, 118.

in Thyatira, and they were suppling her with the purple fabrics to sell.

In addition to purple fabrics, Thyatira was famous for its highly organized trade guilds. There were trade guides for coppersmiths, bronze workers, tanners, leather workers, dyers, workers in wool and linen, potters, bakers, slave dealers and so forth.[119]

The difficulty these trade guides posed for believers was that each trade guild was "inseparably intertwined"[120] with its guardian god. Hendrickson details out the implications of this for a believer:

> These trade Guilds were associated with the worship of tutelary deities; each Guild had its guardian god. The situation, therefore, was somewhat as follow: if you wish to get ahead in this world, you must belong to a guild; if you belong to a guild, your very membership implies that you worship its god. You would be expected to attend the guild festivals and to eat food, part of which is offered to the tutelary deity in which you receive on your table as a gift from the god. And then, when the first feast ends, and the real – grossly immoral – fun begins, you must not walk out unless you desire to become the object of ridicule and persecution! [121]

---

[119] Blake and Edmonds, *Biblical Sites in Turkey*, 132.
[120] Mounce, *The Book of Revelation*, 101.
[121] Hendrickson, *More than Conquerors,* 71

It is into this difficult context that Jesus spoke these words to the church at Thyatira in Revelation 2:18-29:

"And to the angel of the church in Thyatira write: 'The words of the Son of God, who has eyes like a flame of fire, and whose feet are like burnished bronze. I know your works, your love and faith and service and patient endurance, and that your latter works exceed the first.

But I have this against you, that you tolerate that woman Jezebel, who calls herself a prophetess and is teaching and seducing my servants to practice sexual immorality and to eat food sacrificed to idols. I gave her time to repent, but she refuses to repent of her sexual immorality. Behold, I will throw her onto a sickbed, and those who commit adultery with her I will throw into great tribulation, unless they repent of her works, and I will strike her children dead. And all the churches will know that I am he who searches mind and heart, and I will give to each of you according to your works.

But to the rest of you in Thyatira, who do not hold this teaching, who have not learned what some call the deep things of Satan, to you I say, I do not lay on you any other burden. Only hold fast what you have until I come. The one who conquers and who keeps my works until the end, to him I will give authority over the nations, and he will rule them with a rod of iron, as when earthen pots are broken in pieces, even as I myself have received authority from my Father. And I will give him the morning star. He who has an ear, let him hear what the Spirit says to the churches.' "

Jesus begins his message to the church by reassuring them that He is the one who knows them. He commends them for their persevering witness in the city. Jesus personally knew their works, love, faith, service, and patient endurance. He knew how this church was responding in faith to the Gospel and how their faith was working itself out in love. They had maintained a faithful witness in their community. They continued to make progress so that their latter works exceed the first.

Yet, in addition to these kind observations there was a "but" in Jesus' words to the church. He had something serious against them. They were tolerating the women Jezebel,[122] who called herself a prophetess. Jezebel was claiming divine authority for her teaching. She promoted herself as someone who authoritatively spoke for God, even though her teachings contradicted the word of God.

Her teaching was seducing those in the church to compromise with the idolatrous aspects of their city. She was engaging in and advocating for the practice of sexual immorality and the eating of food sacrificed to idols. The leadership at the church was tolerating her teachings and giving her a platform where she was able to promote her alternative views of what the Scriptures taught.

---

[122] Could be her real name or that Jesus is calling her by the nick name Jezebel to identify her with the infamously evil queen Jezebel from 1 and 2 Kings, who fostered in Israel the idolatrous worship of Baal.

Jesus gave the church two courses of action. First, they needed to repent of their actions. If not, consequences would follow. The divine judge,[123] "the one who has eyes like a flame of fire, seeing all things ... His feet are like burnished bronze,"[124] signifying His strength and holiness, will punish the evil doers.

Jesus speaks directly and clearly. If Jezebel does not repent, her bed will become a sickbed, her children will be killed and those who embrace her immoral teaching will be thrown into great tribulation.

Secondly, and more foundationally, they needed to determine which authority they were going to trust. Jesus identifies Himself as the one with supreme authority. Unlike the Emperor or Apollo Tyrimnos (the divine guardian of the city and patron of the guilds),[125] who both claimed to the be the divine sons of Zeus, Jesus alone is truly the son of God. We hear echoes of God the Father saying, "This is my beloved son, listen to Him."[126]

The church at Thyatira needed to grasp that the divine judge, the one who searches the mind and the heart, is the one with the authority to determine true doctrine. Those who

---

[123] The Father has committed all judgment to the son. John 5:22.

[124] In antiquity, bronze was an alloy of copper and tin. Bronze, in a city with bronze workers, would have been a common site and its residents would have been familiar with properties of strength and its purity when refined by fire.

[125]Mounce, *The Book of Revelation*, 191.

[126] See the baptism and transfiguration passages in the gospels.

authoritatively advocate and pursue a different doctrine will face divine punishment.

These believers needed to reject the teaching of "the deep things of Satan." They also must stop neglecting church discipline. They needed to hold fast to the Gospel and keep engaging in Jesus' works till the end.

They were not to base their life on the bogus authority of false teachers and their false teachings. Instead, they were to base their life on the Gospel and the teachings of Scripture, "the deep things of God."[127] If they did this, then the divine judge will reward them with authority and position in His new kingdom.

The problem in this church arose from competing authorities. Paul and the apostles taught the church orthodox doctrine. As early as Acts 15, the church elders agreed that participating in the worship of idols by eating meat offered to them and practicing sexual immorality were wrong. It could not be any clearer.

The church at Thyatira had a choice to make. Were they going to submit to the apostolic teaching or to the competing authority, the prophetess named Jezebel? Jezebel claimed she had a new revelation from God that made eating meat offered

---

[127] 1 Corinthians 2:10.

to idols and sexual immorality permissable.[128] It appears she also engaged in both sinful activities as further proof of the truth of her words.

The question for the church was, "Who is right?" Who do you trust to speak for God? The consistent hermeneutic[129] of the apostles and prophets from Genesis onward, or this new prophet and her creative way of reinterpreting the Scriptures? Is God consistent in His doctrine and messaging, or does God change the definition of sin and righteousness as He goes along? The Scriptures are clear, God does not change.[130]

Those in the church who had embraced Jezebel's teaching needed to repent and return to the Scriptures as the authoritative voice of God. To deviate from the church's long held historical-grammatical hermeneutic of interpreting the written word of God is to deviate from God Himself.

So how ought we to pray for a modern-day church like Thyatira, a church that is confused over who has the authority to interpret the Bible?

Again, we start by thanking God for a church that resembles Thyatira. They loved God and their neighbor. This love,

---

[128] One can hear whispers of the UCC marketing lingo "God is still speaking," which followed two thousand years later advocating this same non-biblical view of morality,
[129] Hermeneutics is the theory and methodology of interpretation.
[130] One brief example: the book of Revelation closes the final chapter with the clear warning to not alter the doctrine of the scriptures.

combined with their faith, moved them to action. Jesus commends them for their good deeds and service. They continued to minister as evidenced by their patient endurance, and their current deeds were even better than their first ones.

Yet, we need to pray for this type of church to rediscover biblical authority and for them to make the Bible the basis for deciding what they should be doing. To go deep, once again, in Scripture and grasp the depth and breadth of the Gospel.

Pray for those in the church to also realize there is a limit to tolerance in the Scriptures. Pray for the church to follow Paul's model for the manner of addressing competing authorities:

> And the Lord's servant must not be quarrelsome but kind to everyone, able to teach, patiently enduring evil, correcting his opponents with gentleness. God may perhaps grant them repentance leading to a knowledge of the truth, and they may come to their senses and escape from the snare of the devil, after being captured by him to do his will.[131]

Ask God to give the church wisdom to understand that relational tolerance does not equate with doctrinal tolerance. The Scriptures lay out the church's orthodox doctrine and opposes all other false and competing narratives.

We need to pray for the church to learn how God defines righteous thinking and behavior. For them to embrace God's

---

[131] 2 Timothy 2:24-26

definition of holiness, which is contrary to the world's definition.

Pray for grace for the church to turn from her antinomian (anti-law) doctrines and to grasp that God is going to hold people accountable to the divine law. As the writer of Hebrews taught:

> And just as it is appointed for man to die once, and after that comes judgment, [132]

Pray for the church to embrace the Gospel, the good news of forgiveness in Christ and the call to live a new life. To experience the reality that:

> I have been crucified with Christ. It is no longer I who live, but Christ who lives in me. And the life I now live in the flesh I live by faith in the Son of God, who loved me and gave himself for me.[133]

Pray for the believers to overcome and hold fast by knowing Jesus and living like Jesus. Jesus lived righteously, endured suffering until the end and was resurrected to new life. He calls the church to do the same. If they do, Jesus will give them

---

[132] Hebrews 9:27
[133] Galatians 2:20

the morning star,[134] the privilege of participating in the sovereign reign of Jesus.[135]

Ask God to open the eyes of the church to see that she cannot be open and affirming of false doctrine and turning a blind eye to those church members engaging in open sin. The Pergamum church was serving well, but Jesus is clear that good deeds are not an excuse for false doctrine. It cannot be either/or. It must be both/and. Jesus is calling this church to embrace all of scripture, which leads to personal holiness as well as good deeds of service. Pray that they might forsake this false gospel of doctrinal tolerance.

Father, I pray for those who worship at a church like Thyatira. We ask that you open their eyes to be able to discern who to trust and to grasp who is teaching the truth from your word. For them to have hearts that are humble and submissive to your word. For them to willing place themselves under the authority of the Scriptures, not under the teachings of various men and women who merely claim authority.

We ask you would give the church's leadership boldness in humbly applying church discipline to those teaching doctrines contrary to your revealed word. For the church to grasp that Christ's mission involves conversion and transformation. To

---

[134] Ironically, Balaam prophesied about a "*star*," a powerful ruler who crushes Israel's enemies in Numbers 24:17.
[135] Beale, *The Book of Revelation*, 268-269.

make disciples who are being renewed in the mind so as to prove that the will of God is good, acceptable and perfect.

In addition to your prayer that flows from the meta-narrative of scripture, you can use the prayer chart below for ideas on how to pray for this type of church:

Praying for Confused Churches like Thyatira

Observations	Prayer Ideas
Strengths to be thankful for	• Their works, their love and faith and service and patient endurance. • Their latter works exceed their first.
Weakness that needs addressed	• Tolerating the false prophet Jezebel who taught and seduced church members to participate in: • Idol worship • Sexual immorality
Specific Actions to pray for	• To reject the false prophetess. • To give the written word sole authority over correct doctrine and behavior. • To begin applying church discipline when warranted.

Knowing Jesus better, to see Jesus	• As the divine King with complete dominion and authority. • As the One who will either purify or consume. • As a place of refuge in His strength and purity.
Promise for the church to believe	• That though the nations rule now, they will reign with Christ in His kingdom
For Leadership	• To lovingly confront false doctrine with the truth of scripture.

8 | Nostalgic Churches (Sardis)

7 | Nostalgic Churches (Sardis)

One of the challenges facing all churches is the effort it takes to keep progressing on its mission. It is easy to push hard for a season and then drift into coasting. It is easier to stop fighting the fight and begin to rest on your laurels. Being on mission requires a constant act of the will. It is simply easier once the church is established to let the mission go and to take comfort in the successes of the past.

How is the church to move forward when it finds it easier to live out of its past, rather than pressing "on toward the goal for the prize of the upward call of God in Christ Jesus?"[136]

Jesus directs his next words to the church at Sardis, or present day Sartmustafa in Turkey. As with others, this city is only mentioned in Revelation three. This church likely began because of Paul's ministry in Asia Minor.[137]

Seven hundred years before the church was founded, Sardis had been one of the greatest cities of Asia Minor. The wealth of Sardis was legendary.

The original city was uniquely located fifteen hundred feet up on one of the rocky spurs of Mount Tmolus. The sides of the

---

[136] Philippians 3:13
[137] Acts 19:10

ridge were smooth with only one steep and difficult approach to the city, making the city impregnable for centuries.

The city considered itself so secure that when the Persian troops finally figured out a way up a fault in the sheer rock face, they found the city completely unguarded. The Sardians had thought themselves too secure to need a guard. Thus, the city of Sardis was easily conquered and fell to the Persians.

The city rebelled against the Persians after two hundred years of control resulting in the Persians besieging the city for two years in response. One night a band of soldiers found a way to climb the steep cliffs once again. When the soldiers got up to the city, again they found no guards. Sardis easily fell back under Persians control a second time because there was no one on watch.[138]

Over time, the top of the plateau was too small to contain the expanding city. The city expanded to the valley beneath the citadel. The city's name "Sardis" is actually a plural noun, since there were functionally two towns, one on the plateau and one in the valley beneath.

In Roman times, Sardis was still very wealthy. Unfortunately, the city was all but destroyed by an earthquake in AD 17. They

---

[138] William Barclay, ed., *The Revelation of John*, vol. 1, 113-115.

were able to rebuild the leveled city thanks to the gracious generosity of the Emperor.

The city became a hub of the Roman highway system in that region. It profited greatly from the extensive trade made possible by the highway system. However, by the time John wrote these words of Jesus, the city was deteriorating and losing influence with Rome. The once great citadel had been abandoned with everyone now living in the valley. The citadel was relegated to being an historical monument at the top of the plateau.

The identity of the Sardians was deeply tied to their past glory. The rebuilt city had the appearance of being thriving and healthy, but it masked an inner decay.[139] The great Sardians, though wealthy, continued to be soft and complacent. Twice, they had lost their city because they were too lazy to place guards on watch. Their soft character was also reflected in the church.

Jesus spoke these words to John for church at Sardis in Revelation 3:1-6:

> "And to the angel of the church in Sardis write: 'The words of him who has the seven spirits of God and the seven stars. I know your works. You have the reputation of being alive, but you are dead. Wake up, and strengthen what remains and is

---

[139] "Sardis," Ronald F. Youngblood, F. F. Bruce, and R. K. Harrison, Thomas Nelson Publishers, eds., *Nelson's New Illustrated Bible Dictionary.*

about to die, for I have not found your works complete in the sight of my God. Remember, then, what you received and heard. Keep it, and repent. If you will not wake up, I will come like a thief, and you will not know at what hour I will come against you.

Yet you have still a few names in Sardis, people who have not soiled their garments, and they will walk with me in white, for they are worthy. The one who conquers will be clothed thus in white garments, and I will never blot his name out of the book of life. I will confess his name before my Father and before his angels. He who has an ear, let him hear what the Spirit says to the churches.' "

Like the city itself, the church was living from its past reputation. Jesus sees beneath their reputation. He reveals that while outsiders might see the church as being alive, He knew they were actually dying. Unfortunately, their identity as a church was tied to their past glory rather than to their present reality. Others might be impressed with them, but Jesus was not.

Unlike the other churches Jesus has addressed, the reason for the struggles in this church was not persecution. Sardis appears to have been quite a peaceful city. Those in the church had been lulled to sleep. They had become lethargic about the radical demands of the Christian faith amid the pagan culture of Sardis.[140] This church needed literally to wake up. They

---

[140] Beale, *The Book of Revelation*, 273

needed to become watchful rather than unprepared and unguarded. Those in the church were not miserable. They were pitiable.[141]

This lack of godly spiritual life unfortunately was also the norm for the members of the church. They thought they were alive but only a dead formalism existed. Jesus exhorts them to repent and strengthen what remains before it is too late. The good news in this critique was that Jesus wanted to revive them.

The other positive thing going for the church was the existence of a small remnant, a few people in the church, who had not soiled their garments with idolatry.[142] Instead, they walked righteously with Jesus. These genuine believers are the only real heartbeat left in the church.

Unfortunately, the others in the church in Sardis were living in such a compromised way that it called into question whether they possessed a true, living faith in Christ. Their unbiblical lifestyle was also compromising the church's Gospel witness in Sardis.

Similar to the theme of the Book of Hebrews, Jesus calls them to prove their faith by waking up, overcoming and persevering in witnessing about Jesus to their city. Jesus explains that their

---

141 Hendrickson, *More than Conquerors,* 77.
142 Stain is used elsewhere in Revelation to refer to the pollution of idolatry and sexual immorality. Revelation 14:4, 6-9, Beale, *The Book of Revelation,* 276

overcoming will prove the genuineness of their faith. This is not in the sense of earning their salvation. Rather their overcoming will be evidence that indeed their faith was real. In the same way, Jesus' worthiness was tied to His overcoming in Revelation 5:9.

> And they sang a new song, saying, "Worthy are you to take the scroll and to open its seals, for you were slain, and by your blood you ransomed people for God from every tribe and language and people and nation."

Jesus began his address to this church by exclaiming that He was the one who has the seven Spirits of God and the seven stars. The seven Spirits refer to the effective working of the Holy Spirit and the seven stars refers to effective working of the word of God.[143] These both together are a portrayal of the heavenly aid Jesus has made available to the church. There is no reason for them to be caught off guard again.

---

[143] The seven Spirits of God were previously referenced in 1:4 and the seven stars in 1:16, 20 and 2:1. The seven Spirits are a figurative designation for the effective working of the Holy Spirit, similar to Zech 4:2-7, [Beale, *The Book of Revelation*, 211]. The mystery of what stars refer to is explained in 1:20. They are the angels of the seven churches. Unfortunately, the mystery is explained with yet another mystery. It could be referring to heavenly angels, as John does in many other parts of the book. Or it could, as I believe, refer to effective working of the biblical message (Angel means messenger) in a manner like how the seven Spirits refers to the working of the Holy Spirit.

So how does one pray for a modern-day church like Sardis, a church that is living in the past while being functionally asleep in the present?

We begin by thanking God that a small remnant still exists in the church who are walking with Jesus. It has been my experience that in many declining New England churches fitting this description of the church at Sardis, there nearly always are a few saints walking with Jesus. They continue to faithfully attend and support the church though it is asleep and dying.

Ask the Holy Spirit to awaken the rest of those attending the church. They need to remember what they had received and heard, i.e. the Gospel of Jesus Christ. Pray for them to embrace the call to believe it and repent, for them to return to a life of faith. Paul says something similar:

> Therefore, as you received Christ Jesus the Lord, so walk in him. [144]

Foundational to every church is the Gospel. Salvation is by faith. Both justification and sanctification come as one places his/her faith in the Gospel. This church needs to repent of their abdication of the Gospel and return to walking by faith in the entirety of Scripture.

---

[144] Colossians 2:6

Pray for this church to have the courage to take an honest assessment of itself. For them to be able to humbly admit that their reputation of the past is not true of the present. That they may be honest and admit that their present deeds have been weighed in the heavenly balances and found wanting. The church needs to embrace the reality that it is on the verge of collapse and what little remains needs to be strengthened.

In the words of Jesus, many of their garments were soiled. Isaiah, many years before Christ, stated it this way:

> We have all become like one who is unclean, and all our righteous deeds are like a polluted garment.[145]

Sardis was known for having the best materials for making clothes. Unfortunately, their spiritual garments were soiled. Pray that they might also be clothed spiritually with fine material of Christ' righteousness. For them to repent and overcome, that Jesus would wash them in His blood and cloth them with white garments.

Pray for God open the eyes of those have fallen asleep spiritually. For them to remember and believe the Scriptures they were taught. Pray and ask the Holy Spirit to fulfill His purpose to convict sinners. Jesus taught that when the Holy Spirit comes, He:

---

[145] Isaiah 64:6

will convict the world concerning sin and righteousness and judgment: concerning sin, because they do not believe in me; concerning righteousness, because I go to the Father, and you will see me no longer; concerning judgment, because the ruler of this world is judged. [146]

Pray for them to not only wake up but to grasp their perilous spiritual state. They need to repent of their hollow spiritual life and their compromised lifestyle. They need to re-engage with the Bible and apply its truths to the way they live their lives. Ask God to give them the grace to be honest with themselves about how their present spiritual life gives more evidence to unbelief than saving faith. For them to either wake up spiritually or come to a living faith in Jesus, so that in end they are not found to be spiritually dead.

Ask God to strengthen the remnant, those who have refused to compromise with idolatry. Ask God to give them boldness to bear testimony to Jesus both in the church and outside the church. For them to be bold in having Gospel conversations with their friends in the church, similar to what Jude admonished the believers in that church to do:

And have mercy on those who doubt; save others by snatching them out of the fire; to others show mercy with fear, hating even the garment stained by the flesh.[147]

---

[146] John 16:8–11.
[147] Jude 22-23

For their boldness to flow from seeing life through the lens of eternity, an eternity with Jesus.

Pray for the church to re-experience the joy which comes from knowing Jesus. For them to come alive and experience that the kingdom of God is peace and joy in the Holy Spirit.[148] Pray that the God of hope would fill them with all joy and peace in believing, so that they would abound in hope by the power of the Holy Spirit.[149]

Father, I pray for churches that are similar to the church in Sardis. Give them the grace to identify where their thinking and their lifestyle are more in line with the world than with your word and to repent. That you might be pleased to save those who are in the church but not yet in your Kingdom. For them to be able to root out and avoid further compromise. For the church to find a renewed boldness in witnessing for Jesus.

In addition to your prayer that flows from the various pages of Scripture, you can the prayer chart below for ideas on how to pray for this type of church:

---

[148] Romans 14:17
[149] Romans 15:13

Praying for Nostalgic Churches like Sardis

Observations	Prayer Ideas
Strengths to be thankful for	• That they were still alive. • For the faithful remnant that has not soiled their garments.
Weakness that needs addressed	• To wake up spiritually. • The church needs an accurate self-assessment, that their garments are soiled. • To live in the present reality rather than the past. To not simply return to what worked in the past. • For the church to strengthen what remains before they die. • To remember the gospel and keep it. • To find their righteousness in Christ.
Specific Actions to pray for	• To return to faith and the scriptures. Or, in some cases, to actually come to faith. • To live by faith and repent • For the Holy Spirit to convict both Christian and non-Christians in the church of sin, righteousness, and

	judgement so as to move them to faith. • For them to walk daily with Jesus. • To overcome sin and temptation by faith.
Knowing Jesus better, to see Jesus	• As the one who provides heavenly aid to the church • As the one who enables them to shine via their witness to those in the dark due to unbelief. • As the one who will confess their names to the Father, if they conquer.
Promise for the church to believe	• To grasp that their eternity is secure as demonstrated by their ability to overcome in the present.
For Leadership	• To lead the return to faith and the Scriptures.

9 | Non-Missional Churches (Philadelphia)

9 | Non-Missional Churches (Philadelphia)

Jesus gave the church a single mission. "Go and Make disciples." Jesus calls every church to be intentionally on mission. Churches are to make a difference in their own community. Each one is to be a light to the Gospel in that small part of the world.

But over time something happens to churches. The mission begins to drift. Less and less time and energy are spent on the mission. More and more focus is placed internally on the church itself. Add to that the fear that often accompanies witnessing and it is easy for the drift to go unchecked. As this drift continues, at some point, the church is functionally no longer on mission. She stops intentionally "going." Those in the community are no longer affected by the Gospel.

How is the church with missional drift to thrive? What is the way forward when the church has turned inward? It is to such a church that Jesus speaks next.

Jesus addresses the church in Philadelphia, the youngest city of the seven mentioned in Revelation. It is located where the borders of ancient Mysia, Lydia and Phrygia met. It is now the modern Turkish city of Alashehir. The city was strategically located on the main route of the Imperial Post from Rome to the East, and was thus referred to as "the Gateway to the East."

The city also had so many temples that it was also referred to as "little Athens."[150]

---

[150] Wiersbe, *The Bible Exposition Commentary*, vol. 2, 578.

The most prominent temple was the temple of Dionysus. Dionysus was the god of wine, fertility, and religious ecstasy.[151] His importance to Philadelphia was centered around the wine industry. There was a great volcanic plain to north of Philadelphia, which was quite fertile and particularly good for growing grapes. The city became famous for great wines. Due to their success in wine-making, Dionysus had become the city's chief pagan cult.[152]

Jesus' opening words to Philadelphia calls the church to be on mission. This call to be local missionaries to the community with the Gospel would have resonated with the residents of Philadelphia.

Most new cities in the ancient world were built by conquering armies as military outposts. However, Philadelphia was uniquely built for civic missionary purposes. The city was founded to evangelize by peaceful means the surrounding area with the Greek culture and the Greek language.

Philadelphia was quite successful in this civic missionary endeavor. So much so that the nearby Lydians had forgotten their own language and were completely Greek-speaking, by AD 19.[153]

There are two other key elements of the city's historical background that were behind the wording of what Jesus said to the church.

---

[151] https://www.britannica.com/topic/Dionysus, accessed 6/9/2020
[152] Mounce, *The Book of Revelation*, 114.
[153] Barclay, *The Revelation of John*, vol. 1, 125.

First, the earthquake in A.D. 17 that destroyed the city of Sardis also devasted Philadelphia. Due to the unique geography of the nearby volcanos, the terrifying aftershocks of the earthquake went on almost daily for years. As a result of this recurring trial, the city soon was referred to as the "city full of earthquakes." Strabo describes this reality:

> Shocks were an everyday occurrence. Gaping cracks appeared in the walls of the houses. Now one part of the city was in ruins, now another. Most of the population lived outside the city in huts and feared even to go on the city streets lest they should be killed by falling masonry. Those who still dared to live in the city were reckoned mad; they spent their time shoring up the shaking buildings and every now and then fleeing to the open spaces for safety. These terrible days in Philadelphia were never wholly forgotten, and people in it ever waited subconsciously for the ominous tremors of the ground, ready to flee for their lives to the open spaces.[154]

Secondly, the city went through a couple of name changes in the first century. Emperor Tiberius was very generous to the city, exempted it from paying taxes and helped financed its rebuilding after it was devastated by the earthquake. In gratitude, they changed the name of the city to Neocaesarea, meaning the "New City of Caesar."

The name was changed again to "Flavia" to honor the new emperor Titus Flavius Vespasianus. However, despite the name changes, most locals continued to refer to the city as

---

[154] Barclay, *The Revelation of John*, vol. 1, 126.

Philadelphia. By the time Revelation was written, the name Philadelphia had been restored.[155]

To the city of Philadelphia, Jesus spoke these words in Revelation 3:7-13:

> "And to the angel of the church in Philadelphia write: 'The words of the holy one, the true one, who has the key of David, who opens and no one will shut, who shuts and no one opens. I know your works. Behold, I have set before you an open door, which no one is able to shut. I know that you have but little power, and yet you have kept my word and have not denied my name.
>
> Behold, I will make those of the synagogue of Satan who say that they are Jews and are not, but lie, behold, I will make them come and bow down before your feet, and they will learn that I have loved you. Because you have kept my word about patient endurance, I will keep you from the hour of trial that is coming on the whole world, to try those who dwell on the earth.
>
> I am coming soon. Hold fast what you have, so that no one may seize your crown. The one who conquers, I will make him a pillar in the temple of my God. Never shall he go out of it, and I will write on him the name of my God, and the name of the city of my God, the new Jerusalem, which comes down from my God out of heaven, and my own new name. He who has an ear, let him hear what the Spirit says to the churches.' "

---

[155] Barclay, *The Revelation of John*, vol. 1, 126.

Jesus has much to commend this church. The church has been faithful to keep Jesus' word despite having little power.

They had not denied Jesus' name. Jesus commends them for patiently enduring opposition from the synagogue of Satan,[156] for some in the Jewish community were severely opposing the Gospel message of Jesus Christ.

In the midst of this opposition from the Jews, Jesus reminds the church that He is the one who is holy, the One who is true, and the One who has the key of David. All which were not true of those of the synagogue of Satan, those who had rejected Jesus. They believed they are children of God but were in truth lying.[157]

Jesus alone is the ultimate Jew, not the so-called Jews of the synagogue. Unlike the Jews who taught the law but could not keep it, Jesus alone is holy because He obeyed all of the law. Unlike the Jews with their various camps of interpretation, Jesus alone both authoritatively taught the truth about the Scriptures and also fulfilled them. Unlike the Jews who assumed they determined who was in God's kingdom,[158] Jesus alone is the one who holds the key, the authority of David to

---

[156] These people may have been Jews in the flesh, but they were not "true Israel" in the New Testament sense (Romans. 2:17–29). Jewish people certainly have a great heritage, but it is no guarantee of salvation (Matthew 3:7–12; John 8:33ff). Wiersbe, *The Bible Exposition Commentary*, vol. 2, , 579.

[157] Matthew 23:15 - Woe to you, scribes and Pharisees, hypocrites, because you travel around on sea and land to make one proselyte; and when he becomes one, you make him twice as much a son of hell as yourselves.

[158] Probably a reference to the practice of the local synagogue of excommunicating Christian Jews. Mounce, *The Book of Revelation*, 116.

determine who is a Jew and who is not. Jesus opens, and no one can shut. He shuts and no one opens.[159]

Jesus will vindicate His church in the future. Jesus will make their Jewish enemies come and bow before their feet. Jesus will make it clear that He loves His church, the true Israel of God which is made up of those with faith in Christ.

The encouraging news is that despite having little power, Jesus has set before them an open door of ministry. Paul often used this phrase "an open door" to describe the ministry.[160] This phrase would have been uniquely relevant for Philadelphia. As we saw above, this border town was founded for the citizens to be missionaries of the Greek culture and language to the surrounding towns.

Plus, God was regularly bringing people to them to hear the gospel. Philadelphia was on the road of the imperial postal service. Caesar's army regularly travelled that road as well as caravans of merchantmen.[161] The church's task was to proclaim Christ to all those God brought to them.

The church of Philadelphia, like the city itself, was founded to be a missional community.

---

[159] These verses allude to Isaiah 22:22, which speaks of one who had David's key to open and shut, indicating full authorization to rule the house. To Jewish Christians excluded from the synagogue, this was Jesus' encouragement that he who rightly ruled the house of David now acknowledged them as his own people. Craig S. Keener, *The IVP Bible Background Commentary: New Testament*, Re 3:7–8.
[160] See 1 Corinthians 16:9, 2 Corinthians 2:12, Colossians 4:3, Acts 14:27.
[161] Barclay, *The Revelation of John*, Vol. 1, 129.

Missional is a Christian term that describes a lifestyle of living as a sent one. Living missionally is to identify with and join God in his mission, which Jesus explained was to seek, to save, to serve others. Those who are living missionally are seeking to do the same in the name of Christ. [162]

This church needed to embrace this mission that Christ had set before them. Yes, they may be personally weak, but the opportunity was great. The church needed to continue to persevere and engage the city with the gospel. The Christians of Philadelphia needed to place their hope of success on God, not on their own strength. God's ultimate victory depends solely upon King Jesus.

Along with this mission came a threefold promise from Jesus. He begins each part of the promise with the words, "I will."

First, in response to their ongoing faithful endurance of keeping Jesus' word, Jesus promises "I will" vindicate them. He will keep them spiritually safe from the future punishment of unbelievers who dwell on the earth. [163]

Secondly, Jesus promises "I will" also make those believers who conquer a pillar in His temple. They will never go out of it. A reassuring promise to those who often fled to the countryside for fear of their lives due to the ongoing

[162] Ed Stetzer, What is a missional church?, Ed Stetzer - Lifeway Research Blog, Lifeway Research, http://www.edstetzer.com/2010/02/what-is-a-missional-church.htm, accessed on February 3, 2010.
[163] Beale, *The Book of Revelation*, 290.

earthquakes. Their future would be safe and secure in God's temple.

Lastly, Jesus promises "I will" give those in Christ a new name and a new identity as sons and daughters of God. The city of Philadelphia had changed its own name twice to honor emperors in gratitude for favor shown to the city. Here Christ, the one who has showered them with favor, changes their name to honor them.

So how does one pray for such a church who needs to re-engage wholeheartedly with the mission? Again, we begin with thanksgiving. Praise God that the church has kept the Jesus' words and has not denied the name of Jesus despite pressure from their community. Thank God that the church is finding her identity in Jesus and His love for them regardless of personal cost.

Ask God to give the church a renewed heart for mission. Pray for them to see where God has opened a door to the church for fruitful ministry. For them to embrace this call to expand Jesus' kingdom. Ask God to give the church grace to move forward on mission knowing that the gates of hell cannot overpower the church.

For the church to be motivated by how even unbelievers, like those in Philadelphia, can change the culture of whole cities via kind missionary engagement. For them to be bold in kindly engaging others with the Gospel. For each member to see how much can accomplish by sharing the Gospel, which has the power to change lives.

Pray for the church to be ok with having little power in the world's eye. For them not to lose heart despite opposition.[164] Ask for them to rely instead on Jesus' power and the power of His word, which is able to penetrate hard rocky hearts with the truth of the Gospel. For them to rest in Jesus' ordained pace of ministry growth. For Jesus opens and no one shuts, he shuts and no one opens.

Pray that they would continue to keep Jesus' words with patient endurance, asking God to keep them from trials. Ask that they would hold onto the promises of Jesus, living with eternity in mind where all will be well.

Father, we pray for modern-day churches that are like the church at Philadelphia. For those in these churches that know you to be moved to greater gospel engagement with their community. For them to keep persevering rather than pull back and only do what is minimal. For the church to become mission-oriented and to walk through the open door that Jesus has set before them. For them to seek the safety of eternity rather than look for security on earth.

In addition to your prayer based on the models of prayer in Scripture, you can use the prayer chart below for ideas on how to pray for this type of church:

---

164 2 Corinthians 4:16-28

Praying for Non-Missional Church like Philadelphia

Observations	Prayer Ideas
Strengths to be thankful for	• That they have Jesus' words and did not deny His name. • For their obedience to Jesus' words with patient endurance. • How their own history enlightens Jesus' calling and ministry.
Weakness that needs addressed	• They have little power.
Specific Actions to pray for	• To embrace the gospel mission that Jesus has sent before them. • To continue to live with patient endurance. To trust Christ's ability to protect them spiritually and enable them to endure. • For the promises of Jesus to comfort and empower them in the gospel ministry to their city. • To overcome by faith. To press on towards the goal for the prize of the upward call of God in Christ Jesus (Philippians 3:14)

Knowing Jesus better, to see Jesus	• As the Holy One. • As the One who holds power over life and death. • As the one who has given them the mission and an open door. • As the one who can protect them spiritually when tribulation comes. • As the one will reward them for conquering.
Promise for the church to believe	• For their future fellowship and identification with Christ in His heavenly kingdom.
For Leadership	• To lead the church to be on mission for Christ in their community.

10 | Worldly Churches (Laodicea)

10 | Worldly Churches (Laodicea)

Central to the church being on mission is the transformation of those in the church. A transformed life is a powerful witness to the truth of the Gospel. A church full of transformed people is hard to write off as a fluke.

Jesus put an exclamation point on this reality when He said that:

> By this all people will know that you are my disciples, if you have love for one another.[165]

The Gospel claims to be transformative in all of life. When those in the church are not being transformed by the gospel, it presents a serious credibility problem to the mission. How is the church to reach those in the community when there is no apparent difference between those in the church and those outside the church?

Why should those in the community believe the Gospel message, if those in the church find it to be so powerless? It to such a situation that Jesus speaks to next.

The final church that Jesus addresses is the one in Laodicea. The church in Laodicea is referenced several times in Paul's letter to the Colossians. Laodicea lies about 40 mile east of Ephesus and 10 mile west of Colossae. The city, known today

---

[165] John 13:35

as Eski Hissar in Turkey, had been a bustling cosmopolitan city in the days of Rome. However, it declined over the centuries and was finally abandoned in the 1400's. Much of what was left of the city was removed and used for building a railway and the nearby Turkish town of Denizili.[166]

The reason for Laodicea's early success was that Rome rebuilt the ancient roads of Asia Minor when they conquered the region. Thus, Laodicea became the major hub for traffic heading west towards Ephesus, or south to the Mediterranean, or east towards southern Galatia, or north and west to Philadelphia, Pergamum and Smyrna. The roads coming out of Laodicea went to all the key cities in Asia Minor and to the east. It was an economic gold mine.

As a result, the city became very wealthy. So wealthy in fact that when the city was destroyed by a massive earthquake in the region in AD 60, the city proudly refused any monetary aid from the Roman government. They paid all the costs to rebuild the city themselves.[167]

The city was unique in that its location had been determined by the road system rather than natural resources. The one negative implication of this was that the city had no natural source of water. Their creative solution to the lack of water

---

[166] G. L. Borchert, "Laodicea," *The International Standard Bible Encyclopedia,* 73.
[167] Borchert, "Laodicea," *The International Standard Bible Encyclopedia,* 73.

was to build a great water system, which was feed by an aqueduct from the nearby springs about 6 miles to the south.

The aqueduct was built from large, tightly fitted, and cemented rectangular stones. They bore through the center of each stone to create a circular central channel. The mountain spring water was transported by the aqueduct to a tall water-distribution tower in Laodicea by syphon action.[168]

The population of Laodicea was cosmopolitan. There were Roman colonizers, the original Phrygians, immigrant Syrian settlers, and many Jews. The deities worshiped in Laodicea reflected this varied background of its citizens.[169]

To the city of Laodicea, Jesus spoke these words in Revelation 3:14-22:

> "And to the angel of the church in Laodicea write: 'The words of the Amen, the faithful and true witness, the beginning of God's creation. I know your works: you are neither cold nor hot. Would that you were either cold or hot! So, because you are lukewarm, and neither hot nor cold, I will spit you out of my mouth. For you say, I am rich, I have prospered, and I need

---

[168] The siphon effect leverages atmospheric pressure to push liquid up while gravity pulls the liquid down. Water always flows from an area under higher pressure to an area of lower pressure, even if the direction is up, as was the case in Laodicea.

[169] Borchert, "Laodicea," *The International Standard Bible Encyclopedia*, 73.

nothing, not realizing that you are wretched, pitiable, poor, blind, and naked.

I counsel you to buy from me gold refined by fire, so that you may be rich, and white garments so that you may clothe yourself and the shame of your nakedness may not be seen, and salve to anoint your eyes, so that you may see. Those whom I love, I reprove and discipline, so be zealous and repent.

Behold, I stand at the door and knock. If anyone hears my voice and opens the door, I will come into him and eat with him, and he with me. The one who conquers, I will grant him to sit with me on my throne, as I also conquered and sat down with my Father on his throne. He who has an ear, let him hear what the Spirit says to the churches.' "

Again, the backdrop of Jesus' words is this cosmic reality that He is present. He knows their deeds. Unfortunately, in this case Jesus is most displeased with their deeds.

The church's deeds were as repulsive as lukewarm water. Lukewarm water was something with which everyone in Laodicea was familiar. The city's elaborate aqueduct delivered fresh stream water to the city. However, by the time the water arrived from the mountains to the city, the water temperature was lukewarm, unrefreshing, and hard to drink.

People prefer for their water to be either cold or hot. Both hot and cold temperatures are refreshing and delightful to the taste buds. Lukewarm water, not so much. The deeds of the

Laodicean church, like lukewarm water, were lackluster and unfulfilling. Jesus' reaction to their deeds was a desire to spit them out of his mouth.

Not only were their deeds lukewarm, but the church was also clueless to this reality. They thought their spiritual state mirrored their financial state. Those in the church were under the belief that they were rich, wealthy, and in need of nothing. They falsely thought that things were actually great.

Jesus enlightens them to their present reality. No, they were not great. They were actually wretched, miserable, poor, blind, and naked. Their financial investments had failed to reap spiritual dividends. They needed to humble themselves and make some better spiritual investments.

Jesus advises them on the needed spiritual investments. First, they were to buy from Him gold refined by fire, a true and abiding faith, so that they could become rich. Second, they were to obtain white garments[170] so that they could clothe themselves with forgiveness to cover the shame of their sin. Thirdly, they needed eye salve[171] to anoint their eyes so that they could see spiritually.

---

[170] Among its chief exports were costly, seamless garments woven of glossy, black wool, which Ramsay suggested may have been behind the reference to "white garments" in Revelation. 3:18. [Borchert, "Laodicea," *The International Standard Bible Encyclopedia,* 78]

[171] The city also the home to a medical school that was famous for its eye salve [Nelson's New Illustrated Bible Dictionary, 1995]. A key ingredient was

The problem with the church was that their whole approach to walking with God was bankrupt. What they valued, the results they were seeking and the means of getting them were not built on the revealed word of God. Rather, they were all grounded in the world's system. Their lack of biblical insight led to poor spiritual eyesight.

Their lukewarm attitude toward religion extended beyond Christianity to the imperial cult as well. Their refusal of an imperial benefaction to help rebuild the city after the earthquake was unusual. It turned the typical relationship with the emperor on its head. It was a not-so-subtle thumbing of their nose at those in power. It all pointed to a lukewarmness in that relationship as well.[172] They were proudly independent. They did not need anyone else. Not the emperor, not even God.

Jesus' rebukes such wrong thinking in the church. Though, His reproof flows from a heart of love. He encourages the church to be zealous and repent. He desires that they follow His example. He pleads with them to overcome and sit down with Him on His throne.

"Phrygian powder," ground locally in Laodicea, apparently was used to treat diseases of the eyes. { Borchert, "Laodicea," *The International Standard Bible Encyclopedia*, 73]

[172] David A. deSilva, "The 'Image of the Beast' and the Christians in Asia Minor: Escalation of Sectarian Tension in Revelation 13," *Trinity Journal* 12, no. 2, 194.

Jesus is not distancing himself from the church, rather instead He stands at the door and knocks. If anyone hears His voice and opens the door, Jesus will enter and sit down with them to dine together. In other words, Jesus will join them in living life together. Jesus is encouraging them:

> Oh, taste and see that the LORD is good! Blessed is the man who takes refuge in him![173]

Jesus longs for them to experience what David experienced:

> O God, you are my God; earnestly I seek you; my soul thirsts for you; my flesh faints for you, as in a dry and weary land where there is no water.[174]

As Augustine so aptly said:

> For you made us for yourself, and our hearts are restless until they find rest in you.[175]

Notice the depth of decline in the church of Laodicea. Jesus addresses the faithful remnant in the church Thyatira. Jesus speaks of a few names who had not spoiled their garments in the church at Sardis. However, in Laodicea Jesus has no one to commend. All Jesus can do is appeal to the whole church to zealously repent.

---

[173] Psalm 34:8
[174] Psalm 63:1.
[175] Augustine, *Confessions*, *Xxxvii [38]*.

There is no commendation from Jesus for any attempt made by anyone in the church to remain faithful to "the testimony of Jesus." They had all caved in the face of economic opportunity and social pressure from the citizens of Laodicea.[176]

The boundary between the Christian community and the rest of the citizens of Laodicea seemed non-existent. The church and community looked and behaved the same. This blurring of the distinctions between the church community and the society at large had led to a functional absorption of the church community into the society.[177]

The church was not making disciples. She was no longer helping believers to engage the Gospel, to wrestle with their faith and teaching them how to live out their counter-cultural identity as Jesus followers. Thus, their message was no longer distinctive, nor attractive.

Jesus begins his address to the church by describing Himself as the Amen, the faithful and true Witness, the Beginning of the creation of God. Jesus is the beginning of the new creation, the first born from the dead.[178] The church at Laodicea

---

[176] deSilva, "The Social Setting of the Revelation to John: Conflicts Within, Fears Without," 292.
[177] deSilva, "The Social Setting of the Revelation to John: Conflicts Within, Fears Without," 298.
[178] Colossians 1:15, 18, Romans 1:5.

desperately needed to participate in the new creation brought about by the death and resurrection of Jesus.[179]

Unfortunately, Paul's description of an unbeliever aptly describes those who attended the Laodicean church.

> And you were dead in the trespasses and sins in which you once walked, following the course of this world, following the prince of the power of the air, the spirit that is now at work in the sons of disobedience, among whom we all once lived in the passions of our flesh, carrying out the desires of the body and the mind, and were by nature children of wrath, like the rest of mankind.[180]

So how ought we pray for a worldly church like Laodicea? A church that looks and acts like the worldly community where they live. A church that has lost the message of Christ and feels no remorse for not living a life of holiness that reflects Jesus Christ. A church whose gospel message is no longer distinctive, nor attractive.

---

[179] Isaiah. 65:15–16 stands behind the title "the Amen, the faithful and true," as well as behind the concluding "the beginning of the creation of God." The notion of God and of Israel as a "faithful witness" to the new creation in Isa. 43:10–12 forms the background for "witness." Isa. 65:15–16 stands behind the title. This allusion is used to indicate that Christ is the divine "Amen, the faithful and true witness" to his own resurrection as "the beginning of the new creation of God," in inaugurated fulfillment of the Isaianic new-creation prophecies [see Beale, *The Book Of Revelation,* 1996 plus Beale and McDonough, "Revelation," in *Commentary on the New Testament Use of the Old Testament,* 1097–1098.]
[180] Ephesians 2:1–3

Unfortunately, the only things to be thankful for about this type of church is that they have somehow managed to remain a church, albeit just barely, and for Jesus' gracious attitude towards the church. They deserve to be spit out of Jesus' mouth but instead Jesus continues to pursue them relationally. Jesus is outside knocking on the door asking to come in. Astonishingly, Jesus is rooting for them to repent and re-engage with Him.

A key prayer need for this type of church is to gain an accurate spiritual self-assessment and to apply the Gospel remedy to their ill-health. They need God's grace to be able to discern just how badly their spiritual lives are going.

> Augustine's first principle of prayer is that before you know what to pray for and how to pray for it, you must first become a particular kind of person. "You must account yourself 'desolate' in this world, however great the prosperity of your lot maybe." The scales must have fallen from your eyes and you must see clearly that no matter how great your earthly circumstances become, they can never bring you the lasting peace, happiness, and consolation that are found in Christ.[181]

Pray for those in this church to see through new eyes the poor state of their souls and the precarious state of their relationship with Jesus. They run the risk of Jesus spitting

---

[181] Timothy Keller, *Prayer*, 84.

them out of His mouth. Instead, they need to run to Jesus for forgiveness and new birth.

Pray that they are zealous to repent. Pray for them to respond to Jesus' knocking, to open the door and to engage Jesus relationally. Pray that they would return to faith or come to faith.

Pray for them to develop an eternal perspective on what is truly valuable. Ask that they grasp what is true wealth. To seek from Jesus gold refined by fire, that is, a true and abiding faith.[182] For them to find their confidence in the gospel rather than earthly riches and success. For the church to be a community of those engaged with Jesus rather than a bland country club for those successful in the world's eyes.

Pray for them to be those who obtain true spiritual wealth from Jesus, and the white garments of forgiveness with which to cover the shame of their sin, and spiritual eye salve by which Holy Spirit might open their eyes to see Jesus.

Pray that this church would be a church who emulates the example of Jesus, the one who overcame and conquered. For those in the church to also be ones who overcome.

Father, we pray for those that attend a church like the one at Laodicea. Open their eyes to see the how great is the

---

[182] 1 Peter 1:7

disconnect between what you say in your word and how they think and act. For them to be able to see how they have accommodated the world rather than submitted to your teachings and serve You.

May they grasp the perilous state of their souls and open the door of their hearts to Jesus. Give them a desire to want to engage relationally with your son. May they live for eternity rather for than for the momentary trinkets of this world.

In addition to your prayers based on scripture, you can use the prayer chart below for ideas on how to pray for this type of church:

Praying for Worldly Church like Laodicea

Observations	Prayer Ideas
Strengths to be thankful for	• Still a church. • Jesus' love for the church.
Weakness that needs addressed	• Their lukewarm deeds. • Their false assessment of how they are doing.
Specific Actions to pray for	• Accurate spiritual self-assessment and discernment. To not despise the Lord's discipline. • To see with new eyes the poor state of their souls and the precarious state of their relationship with Jesus. • For a renewed wholeheartedness in applying all their resources, energy and skills to seeking Jesus and engaging in His kingdom work. • An eternal perspective on what is truly valuable. • To seek from Jesus gold refined by fire, i.e., a true and abiding faith. • To find their confidence in the Gospel rather than earthly riches and success.

	• To be a community of those engaged with Jesus. • To be zealous to repent. • To respond to Jesus' knocking. • To emulate the example of Jesus and be overcomers. • To overcome by faith.
Knowing Jesus better, to see Jesus	• As the one who first overcame, the first born of the new creation. • As the one who will share His throne. • As the one who desires a deep and intimate relationship with them.
Promise for the church to believe	• That they will inherit a ruling position with Jesus.
For Leadership	• To lead the church in repenting of their lukewarmness towards Jesus.

11 | Praying for Individual Churches

11 | Praying For Individual Churches

It is my prayer that as you pray for Christ's church, you would also personally encounter the living God in a new way for yourself. For your own heart to beat more after God. For you to experience what Augustine experienced as He sought God's face:

> You called and cried out loud and shattered my darkness. You were radiant and responded, you put to flight my blindness. You were fragrant, and I drew my breath and now pant after you. I tasted you, and I feel but hunger and thirst for you. You touched me, and I am set on fire to attain the peace which is yours.[183]

It is my prayer that as God's people pray for the church, they would also desire more of what God desires, for His church to thrive.

Each the seven churches in Revelation were faced with some difficult choices. Would they remain faithful to their charge? Would they hold fast to the name of Jesus amid the darkness of the world? Would they be the lampstands they were called to be? Would their light burn bright, or would it continue to diminish? Would the tiny flicker of light left in some of the churches simply go out?[184]

Each of these churches constantly faced the temptation to stop listening to Christ and instead listen to the world. Satan pressured these churches with persecution, false teachers,

---

[183] Augustine, *Confessions* Xxxvii [38], 201.
[184] Hendrickson, *More than Conquerors,* 79.

competing false narratives of what is true worship, and plentily of opportunities to engage their sinful passions.

Not much has changed today. Yet by God's grace, there is still a church on earth. However, she needs our prayers.

Satan has gained a stronghold in many churches, especially here in New England. We must fight on our knees for each church's repentance and growth. These churches need God to open their ears to hear the truth of Scripture, and for the Holy Spirit to give them a heart to repent and believe.

The church will only move in the direction of thriving again when God's word begins to reign in their hearts and minds:

> For though we walk in the flesh, we are not waging war according to the flesh. For the weapons of our warfare are not of the flesh but have divine power to destroy strongholds. We destroy arguments and every lofty opinion raised against the knowledge of God, and take every thought captive to obey Christ. [185]

Each church is the same, and yet each church is unique. Where possible, it is helpful when praying for a particular church to understand that church's own individual context, both internally and externally, as well as its history.

As we saw in the previous chapters, Jesus framed his words to each individual church using language that fit that church's context. The more you know about the context of a church, the

---

[185] 2 Corinthians 10:3–5

more informed can be your prayers. This will allow you to pray more specifically for the various needs of that church.

Where this is most practical is with your own church. Thus, begin with praying for our own church. You know your church the best and, therefore, you can be very specific in your prayers. As you ask Jesus to intercede on your own church's behalf, you can drill down to even individual needs because you know the people of your own church.

You also need to pray for other churches in your area. Both the healthy churches and the unhealthy churches. In the 2010 US census, there was almost 8,000 churches registered in New England. Many of those are in serious decline and mirror one of the seven churches in Revelation.

Fortunately, you can still pray intelligently for the individual churches around you, even those you know little about, using this framework from Revelation 2 and 3. All you need to know is a little about the health of the church and its denomination.

This is possible because the churches in Revelation also show us the different phases in the lifecycle of a church as it drifts away from the gospel and wonders down the road of declining spiritual health.

These words of Jesus are to different churches, yet you can also see them as photographs of any church at various points in its lifecycle, from maturity towards eventual death.

The flow of decline in Revelation two and three would then be as follows: [186]

Ephesians: Cooling of the Heart, declining Love for Jesus.

Smyrna :   A devaluing of wholehearted commitment to Christ. Is God worth the trouble?

Pergamum: Competing Doctrines. Sinful practices now appear in the shape of an article of faith, allowing evil greater inroads and the ability to diversify.

Thyatira: Competing Authority. False prophets/teachers arise with competing claims of truth. There is a growing influence of those departing from the Gospel and misusing authority.

Sardis: Syncretism. What was received and heard is no longer remembered and held. Beliefs from various belief systems are merged together.

Philadelphia: Nominalism. Only pockets of missional activity remain.

Laodicea: Accommodation. The world and the church look the same.

The problem of decline starts in the hearts of its members and ends up with members of the church being indistinguishable from the world.

In the first four churches, the progress of decline is driven by consolidation and concentration of power, with all its abuses. In the last three churches, sin and error move the church to doctrinal disintegration, separation, and individualism. The end result is that each church becomes their own version of "church", untethered to Jesus.

The sad reality is that this progression shows the church in the process of conversion to the world, instead of the world in the process of conversion to Christ, by means of the church. [187]

Thus, the tone and style of Jesus' words changes in response to the increasing decline of the church He addresses. There is a growing sense of urgency and concern. To the first three churches, Jesus encourages them to listen and gives a promise to those who will overcome. To the next three churches, Jesus gives a promise for those who will overcome and then confronts the believers to listen. To the last church, Jesus is standing outside at the door knocking, unsure if anyone will even listen. If anyone does listen and overcome there is a promise.[188]

The call to revitalization is the same for each church in Revelation but the starting point gets increasingly worse. There is no magic formula to apply but the pattern is the same.

---

[187] Seiss, *Lectures on the Apocalypse,* Vol 1, 189.
[188] Seiss, *Lectures on the Apocalypse,* Vol 1, 186-188.

The church must listen to Jesus, believe His promises and overcome by faith. We need to pray accordingly.

Unfortunately, history show us how Jesus, the husband of the church, often fades out of the church's view. Without Jesus, the church becomes self-satisfied, sinning more boldly but internally empty like the world.

A declining church needs us to pray for it to re-encounter Jesus. We need, like the apostle Paul, to keep asking the Father for such a church to be empowered to know Jesus better.[189]

It can be quite discouraging when one looks around at the state of the thousands of churches in the US, especially in New England. The majority have shifted theologically from the Gospel and have embraced the value system of the world. They have drifted missionally from the call to make disciples of Jesus, to wanting to make disciples of a various political movements. Movements, which though rooted in Judeo-Christian doctrine, have rejected those same doctrines.

The great need is prayer. Let us ask the Holy Spirit to do the heart work Jesus promised:

> And when He (the Holy Spirit) comes, He will convict the world concerning sin and righteousness and judgment: concerning sin, because they do not believe in me; concerning righteousness, because I go to the Father, and you will see me no longer;

---

189 Ephesians 1:15-18

concerning judgment, because the ruler of this world is judged.[190]

The great need of our churches today is the same as those churches Jesus spoke to in Revelation. They need to hear and listen to Jesus. They need to believe the promises of Jesus. They need to overcome by faith.

Satan is always at work attempting to move the church in the direction of decline and ultimately to deny Jesus. Sometimes his schemes are obvious, but many times they are currents flowing beneath the surface. Like rip tides that cannot be seen from the shore but will nevertheless drag you out to sea if you get caught in them.

Churches need God's grace to truly see the current state of their church and to humbly apply the gospel remedy. Like Paul, pastors and leaders must be:

> determined to know nothing among you except Jesus Christ, and Him crucified.[191]

Pastors need to wisely apply the gospel to their particular church's problems as Paul did at Corinth. Yet, without prayer, the competing voices often gain the upper hand. The world's promises seem to offer a greater reward at a lower personal cost.

Jesus calls the church to view life through the lens of eternity. The world's rewards may come faster, but they are trinkets

---

[190] John 16:8–11
[191] 1 Corinthians 2:1–2

compared to what God has in store for the church in eternity. The present cost to following Jesus is but a light momentary affliction when viewed in the light of God's promises for eternity.[192]

Paul, one of the hardest working kingdom laborers the church has ever known, was dependent on prayer for the success of his ministry. Paul's letters consistently show us his commitment to prayer:

> As we night and day keep praying[193]

> We give thanks to God, the Father of our Lord Jesus Christ, praying always for you, [194]

> To this end also we pray for you always[195]

> But about midnight [from in jail] Paul and Silas were praying and singing hymns of praise to God[196]

> always offering prayer with joy in my every prayer for you all, [197]

He was also regularly asking the churches to pray for him:

> Brethren, pray for us. [198]

---

[192] 2 Corinthians 4:17-18
[193] 1 Thessalonians 3:10
[194] Colossians 1:3
[195] 2 Thessalonians 1:11
[196] Acts 16:25
[197] Philippians 1:4
[198] 1 Thessalonians 5:25

Pray on my behalf[199]

Prayer is integral to the church being able to fulfil the mission. We need laborers for Christ's church to be hard working in all aspects of Christ's mission, including the hard work of prayer. For them to embrace the reality that unless the Lord builds the house those who labor, build in vain.[200]

Reversing the course of a church's decline and leading her to become a thriving flourishing church is neither quick, nor is it easy. The good news is that both Scriptures and history show us that God is the God of renewal. God delights to revive His people.

For renewal to become a reality, we need to pray for the church to believe what Jesus, the living word, has spoken through his written word. For it is only with the eyes of faith that the church can recognize its error and right its course.

Renewal begins when the church stops and listens to the one voice that matters, the voice of her husband, Jesus Christ. As in real life, it is never worth it to gain everything else and lose your marriage. Pray that the church would wholeheartedly pursue her husband, Jesus Christ.

The great news is that Jesus Himself is also praying for the church. Our great mediator and intercessor is personally praying for the church.[201] Jesus loves His bride. May we also

---

199 Ephesians 6:18–19
200 Psalm 127:1
201 1 Timothy 2:5, Hebrews 7:25.

show our love for the church by praying for her. It will take work and effort but that is what love does.

We have the great privilege of participating in the mission of Christ through prayer. The need of the hour for churches is prayer, especially for the churches of New England. Please join me in praying for Christ's church in your surrounding area.

You can use the prayer guides at the end of each chapter to help direct your prayers for the various types of churches that dot the landscape of New England and elsewhere around the world. These guides can also be downloaded for free at www.overseed.org\PrayForChurches.

May God bless you as you intercede for Jesus' church!

Bibliography

Appleton, George ed. *The Oxford Book of Prayer.* Oxford, England; Oxford University Press, 1985.

Augustine, Saint, *Confessions,* Oxford, England; Oxford University Press, 1991.

Barclay, William, ed., "The Revelation of John," vol. 1, *The Daily Study Bible Series*, Philadelphia: The Westminster John Knox Press, 1976.

Barrett, C.K., *A Critical and Exegetical Commentary on the Acts of the Apostles*, Vol 2, Edinburgh: T. and T. Clark, 1998.

Beale, G.K., "The Book of Revelation," in *The New International Greek Testament Commentary*, Grand Rapids: Eerdmans Publishing Company, 1999.

Beale, G. K. and McDonough, Sean M, "Revelation," in *Commentary on the New Testament Use of the Old Testament* Grand Rapids, MI; Nottingham, UK: Baker Academic; Apollos, 2007.

Bennet, Arthur, *The Valley of Vision: A Collection of Puritan Prayers & Devotions,* Carlisle, PN: The Banner of Truth Trust, 1975.

Blake, Everette and Edmonds, Anna, *Biblical Sites in Turkey*, London: Milet Publishing, 2002.

Borchert , G. L., "Laodicea," ed. Geoffrey W Bromiley, *The International Standard Bible Encyclopedia, Revised.* Wm. B. Eerdmans, 1979–1988.

Chisholm, Hugh, ed. "Neocorate". *Encyclopedia Britannica (11th ed.).* Cambridge: Cambridge University Press, 1911.

Criswell, W. A., *Expository Sermons on Revelation*, Vol 2. Grand Rapids, MI: Zondervan Publishing House, 1963.

deSilva, David A., "The 'Image of the Beast' and the Christians in Asia Minor: Escalation of Sectarian Tension in Revelation 13," *Trinity Journal* 12, no. 2, 1991.

deSilva, David A., "The Social Setting of the Revelation to John: Conflicts Within, Fears Without," *Westminster Theological Journal* 54, no. 2, 1992.

Featherston, William R., *My Jesus, I Love Thee*, 1864.

Ford, J. Massyngberde. *Revelation.* Vol. 38 of *The Anchor Yale Bible Commentary.* Garden City: Doubleday, 1975–1978.

Gloag, Paton James. *A Critical and Exegetical Commentary on the Acts of the Apostles, Volume 2.* T. & T. Clark, 1870.

Harland, Philip. "Sphere of Contention, Claims of Pre-eminence." Pages 53–63 in *Religious Rivalries and the Struggle for Success in Sardis and Smyrna*. Studies in Christianity and Judaism. Edited by Richard S. Ascough. Waterloo, Ontario, Canada: Wilfrid Laurier University Press, 2005.

Henrickson, William, *More than Conquerors, Grand Rapids, MI: Baker Book House, 1940*.

Holland, Tom, *Dominion*, New York: Basic Books, 2019.

Hopkins, Jasper and Richardson, Herbert, translators, *Complete Philosophical and Theological Treatises of Anselm of Canterbury*, Minneapolis; The Arthur J. Banning Press, 2000.

Hunter, James Davison, *How To Change The World*, Oxford: Oxford University Press, 2010.

Keller, Timothy, *Prayer*, New York: Dutton, 2014.

Keener, Craig S., *The IVP Bible Background Commentary: New Testament*, Downers Grove, IL: InterVarsity Press, 1993.

Kraybill, J. Nelson. *Imperial Cult and Commerce in John's Apocalypse*. Journal for the Study of the New Testament: Supplement 132. Sheffield: Sheffield Academic, 1996.

Keener, Craig S. *The IVP Bible Background Commentary: New Testament*. Downers Grove, IL: InterVarsity Press, 1993.

Kempis, Thomas a, *The Imitation of Christ*, Harold C. Gardiner, ed. New York: Image/Doubleday, 1955.

MacGregor, Jim, *Jesus' Words to Seven Churches of Roman Asia*, Self-published by the author.

The Martyrdom of Polycarp, www.earlychristianwritings.com/text/martyrdompolycarp-lake.html, accessed 08.10.2020.

Mounce, Robert H., "The Book of Revelation," in *The New International Commentary on the New Testament*, Grand Rapids: Eerdmans Publishing Company, 1977.

North, R., "Thyatira," ed. Geoffrey W. Bromiley, *The International Standard Bible Encyclopedia*, Grand Rapids: Wm. B. Eerdmans, 1979-1988.

Otttman, Ford C., *The Unfolding of the Ages*, Fincastle, VA: Scripture Truth Book Company, 1905.

Packer, J.I., *Knowing Christianity*, Wheaton, Il: Harold Shaw Publishers, 1995.

Preface of Lent," *The Book of Common Prayer.* New York: The Church Hymnal Corporation, 1979.

Seal, David, "Ephesus," "Smyrna," ed. John D. Barry et al., *The Lexham Bible Dictionary.* Bellingham, WA: Lexham Press, 2016.

Seiss, Joseph, *Lectures on the Apocalypse*, Vol I. New York, NY: Charles C Cook, 1865.

Stetzer, Ed, *What is A Missional* Church, Ed Stetzer - Lifeway Research Blog, Lifeway Research, http://www.edstetzer.com/2010/02/what-is-a-missional-church.html, accessed on February 3, 2010.

Strabo, *The Geography of Strabo. Literally Translated, with Notes, in Three Volumes.*, ed. H. C. Hamilton, Medford, MA: George Bell & Sons, 1903.

Youngblood , Ronald F., Bruce, F. F., and Harrison, R. K., Thomas Nelson Publishers, eds., *Nelson's New Illustrated Bible Dictionary.* Nashville, TN: Thomas Nelson, Inc., 1995.Vives, Ludovicus quoted in George Appleton, ed. *The Oxford Book of Prayer*, Oxford; Oxford University Press, 1985.

Wiersbe, Warren W., *The Bible Exposition Commentary*, vol. 2, Wheaton, IL: Victor Books, 1996.

Bruce Winter, *After Paul Left Corinth, The Influence of Secular, Ethics and Social Change*, Grand Rapids, MI: Erdmans Publishing, 2001.

Zodhiates, Spiros, *The Complete Word Study Dictionary: New Testament.* Chattanooga, TN: AMG Publishers, 2000.

About the Author

Dr. Jim Harrell is president and co-founder of Overseed. He has his Doctor of Ministry in renewal ministries and Masters of Divinity from Gordon-Conwell Theological Seminary. Jim's background is discipleship, mentoring and church planting/revitalization.

Jim came to Christ in the Christian Missionary Alliance church he attended while growing up in Vermont. He was a student leader with The Navigators at UVM , helped start the work at the University of Miami and ministered on staff at the University of TN. After that, God called him out of The Navigators to minister in the local church. He helped with two church plants in Burlington, VT, where he was the unofficial associate pastor of the second church plant.

Jim moved to the Boston area in 1999 to finish seminary and began attending Byfield Parish Church, (a UCC denominational church), which is where he caught the vision of replanting / revitalizing churches. Jim applied his background in church planting, shepherding and training towards developing a plan for this vision. The outcome of that process was the formation of Overseed, Inc.

It is Jim's passion to help declining churches to thrive once again by re-embracing the gospel and by moving out into the community with the message and service of Christ.

CPSIA information can be obtained
at www.ICGtesting.com
Printed in the USA
JSHW040450070521
14434JS00004B/7